Career Paths for the
21st Century

CAREER PATHS FOR THE 21ST CENTURY

HOW TO BEAT JOB INSECURITY

Jim Durcan & David Oates

CENTURY
BUSINESS

Jim Durcan and David Oates have asserted their rights under the Copyright, Designs and Patents Act, 1988, to be identified as the authors of this work.

First published in the United Kingdom by Century Ltd
Random House, 20 Vauxhall Bridge Road, London SW1V 2SA

Random House Australia (Pty) Limited
16 Dalmore Drive, Scoresby,
Victoria 3179, Australia

Random House New Zealand Limited
18 Poland Road, Glenfield
Auckland 10, New Zealand

Random House South Africa (Pty) Limited
PO Box 2263, Rosebank 2121, South Africa

Random House UK Limited Reg. No. 954009

Papers used by Random House UK Limited are natural, recyclable products made from wood grown in sustainable forests. The manufacturing processes conform to the environmental regulations of the country of origin.

Companies, institutions and other organizations wishing to make bulk purchases of any business books published by Random House should contact their local bookstore or Random House direct: The Special Sales Director, Random House, 20 Vauxhall Bridge Road, London SW1V 2SA
Tel: 0171 973 9000 Fax 0171 828 6681

Random House UK Limited Reg. No. 954009

ISBN 0 7126 7607 4

Typeset by Palimpsest Book Production Limited,
Polmont, Stirlingshire
Printed and bound in Great Britain by
Mackays of Chatham plc, Chatham, Kent

Contents

Acknowledgements

Career management is still a very inexact science. Finding a new covenant between employer and employee is taking many different forms and is still pretty much at the experimental stage. With little conclusive evidence to show that new career paths are the way ahead, the authors are doubly grateful that organizations and individuals have been prepared to talk in depth about their theories, practices and achievements. We owe special thanks to those organizations that have been prepared to open their new approaches to scrutiny to provide case studies for this book. They include Shell International, SmithKline Beecham, Sun Life Assurance Society, The Post Office, Hoskyns Group, Trent Regional Health Authority, National Westminster Life Assurance, 3M, Standard Chartered Bank and Sun Microsystems.

We are particularly grateful to IBC UK Conferences who gave us access to material generated by a conference on career planning held in London. Thanks are also due to Future Perfect (Counselling) Ltd for allowing us to draw on material from a landmark report on career development in top UK companies, and to GHN, Drake Beam Morin and Management Career Development, for providing insights into their research in this critical area. Ashridge Management College and *Harvard Business Review* were kind enough to allow us to extract material from articles that throw valuable new light on the subject.

A host of individuals gave generously of their time to elaborate on their experiences and theories. Mandy Johnson of SmithKline Beecham and Steve Harrison of 3M kindly talked to us about their varied careers. Professor Christine Edwards of Kingston Business School addressed the issue of women's careers. David Clutterbuck, a leading management author and expert on mentoring and John O'Brien, a career development counsellor, contributed considerably to the pool of knowledge driving the career development motor forward. Simon Caulkin, writing in *Management Today* and Michael Blakstad, writing in *Director* magazine, kindly gave us permission to extract material from their somewhat controversial articles on subjects related to the theme of this book.

Fiona McLaren of Speechly Bircham, who has helped with previous books, has again been instrumental in setting the authors off on the trail of valuable research. Such assistance is immeasurable.

We hope that the combined impact of all the above contributors has resulted in a book that throws some fresh light on one of the most hotly debated topics in current management circles.

Chapter One
Compensating for Insecurity

A host of turbulent changes in the structures and processes of large organizations means that upwardly mobile managers need more than ever to carve out their own career paths. They need to take charge of their own personal development and training; to develop their own sense of direction. They need to recognize their own values and ensure that these are reflected and fulfilled in their work. They have to create their own career progression rather than rely on corporate human relations departments to chart the course for them. Their careers may embrace many companies or only one – in either case they will need wider experience, more skills and greater competence than their predecessors to rise in their organizations.

The more enlightened companies recognize and communicate that they can no longer guarantee job security. An alternative reward system is needed. Many organizations continue to believe that fatter reward packages and greater benefits will suffice. Others appreciate that to attract and keep the best talent they need to offer 'open market' options and development facilities that improve their managers' employability.

This book outlines the many factors that are leading to a more self-reliant form of career management. It describes and analyses the ways that enlightened companies are helping their employees to prepare themselves for the next career move. Such career moves may be in a very different direction from their current work.

Promoting self-management of careers requires that organizations do more than provide time to pursue skills training outside a manager's current job brief and establish state-of-the-art training aids to encourage self-development. Innovative organizations are reassessing the whole basis of the employment relationship with their managers.

Some are considering the extent to which they should employ managers at all given the opportunities for contracting out whole tranches of the traditional organization. Innovative organizations are seeking new means to meet the growing aspirations of their managers. Simultaneously they are developing structures that are less expensive, more flexible and more responsive to their markets than ever before.

Managers themselves are increasingly realizing that they are operating in an entirely different corporate climate from that of a decade ago. Traditional systems of career planning have been blown away by the sweeping changes, advancing from all directions, that have come in the wake of two severe recessions. Among these changes are:

(a) Corporate restructuring, the flattening of the pyramid, delayering and downsizing

Whatever term you use, the fact of the matter is that in order to survive most companies are having to reorganize the way they do business. For many it has meant cutting out huge swathes of middle management to reduce overheads, and the traditional corporate ladder up the hierarchy has lost many of its rungs. There are fewer jobs to which managers can aspire. The middle management training grounds in which people formerly acquired the knowledge and skills to advance their careers have virtually disappeared. Career progression will never be the same again. It is estimated that around 90 per cent of Britain's largest organizations have restructured in the past five years, nearly half of whom report having noticed increasing demotivation among the workforce.

The old model of career progression for managers was that of the escalator. The major difficulty was fighting your way through the queue at the bottom to secure a place. Thereafter you were carried smoothly upwards and away from those still jostling at its foot. The new model – that of the emergency exit – reflects the impact of a power cut. The escalator has failed. The emergency lights provide little illumination. Those in a hurry are casting about for alternatives – stairways, ladders, ropes, passages and tunnels that would permit them some movement, any movement. Many remain, hoping despite the evidence that 'normal service will be resumed shortly'.

The recession 'survival strategy' adopted by many organizations has resulted in negative effects on employment conditions, according to a survey conducted by the Institute of Management and Clerical

Medical Investment Group. The survey – *Survival of the Fittest* – examined over 1,300 managers' current experiences of, and attitudes to, work. Among the findings were:

- Career direction changes for almost 50 per cent of managers. Almost 40 per cent said they were still trying to cope with their changed circumstances.
- One in three respondents had been in their current role for two years or less.
- Extreme anxiety over job security was expressed by one in five managers.
- Concern about future career opportunities was expressed by 60 per cent of respondents.
- Only 15 per cent of respondents expected their next move to be promotion within their existing organization. Almost three in ten saw their future outside the organization.
- Anxiety about their future financial position was expressed by over 80 per cent of respondents.
- For 80 per cent of respondents workloads had increased over the previous two years. Almost six in ten said their workloads had greatly increased.

The survey results offer some fascinating insights into the extent to which managers have begun to adjust to the new realities. If only 15 per cent expect their next move to be promotion within their existing organization but only 30 per cent see their future outside the organization, that leaves at least 55 per cent who see their next move as lateral inside their existing organization, or no movement at all. The likelihood of no movement is doubtful in a situation where a third of respondents have been in their current job for two years or less. The growth in workloads is obviously difficult for those concerned but it is also indicative of the demands for a wider range of skills and competencies. Those demands provide opportunities for managers prepared to search for alternative career paths.

A recent report by Future Perfect, the London-based consultancy and counselling group for organizations and people in transition, suggests that the major restructuring of companies that has taken place over the past decade may represent the ending of the long-standing informal contract between the employer and the employee. 'This contract offered loyalty and commitment in exchange for security.

3

The downsizing of the last years has done much to erode confidence in that contract, and there is now considerable evidence of high levels of distrust among those still in employment.' The report calls for a new type of relationship to be forged.

Such a perspective obviously applies in those larger organizations that had grown in employment terms and are now shrinking. When organizations grow they grow from the bottom up. New layers are added to the existing organization. Those who join early have all the benefits of the escalator. The faster the organization grows the quicker the escalator and the greater the opportunities. Those who join later contemplate the careers of their managers and expect that theirs will follow a similar path. In reality, once the organization stops growing new opportunities for promotion are reduced to 'dead men's shoes'. If the organization shrinks but the human resources policy is to protect existing long-serving employees then opportunities are further reduced for new and recent entrants.

In contrast, career opportunities in small and growing organizations may still reflect the dynamism and energy of the escalator model. Experience suggests that employment in such organizations is not secure – failure rates among start-up companies remain worryingly high – but in the current climate employment everywhere seems less secure. Smaller organizations, with their looser structures and relative absence of procedures, have always had their attractions for those to whom security was not a key issue. Large corporations are increasingly taking on the market-driven imperative to behave as flexibly and quickly as their smaller rivals. They have to reconsider their whole approach to human resources with its burden of the past and the expectations that were generated.

(b) Cultural change
Companies everywhere are seeking culture changes to align their people's behaviour with the new demands of the market-place and the technological advances that are radically transforming the way they do business. Networking and the delegation of responsibilities to front-line troops are leading to more open systems of management. Organizations that were committed to a strong central direction in pursuit of long-term plans are increasingly revising their priorities. Following the plan is increasingly seen as less relevant than adapting to circumstances. Not being seen to make mistakes is losing ground

to learning from one's mistakes. Entrepreneurialism, risk-taking and innovation are being seen as far more important than keeping one's head down, playing it safe and following procedures. For those who value structure, order and predictability the change provokes a major conflict with their own values and self-image.

(c) Business process re-engineering

Many companies, realizing that they are no longer structured for today's demands are going back to basics and seeking to re-engineer their organizations around their business processes. Detailed analysis by specially formed task forces invariably reveals creaky systems based on out-of-date working practices. Overmanning and long-winded systems between managerial layers that have grown over time and have never been questioned are brought into the daylight and subjected to vigorous review. Ironically, the managers carrying out such reviews are often themselves the first casualties of the realignment. They often preside over their own demise.

Even when times are good, there is likely to be no let up in the drive towards leaner organizations through business process re-engineering (BPR) exercises. Shell recently reduced its service personnel from 7,000 to around 5,500 as a result of reviewing its business processes at a time when trade appeared to be flourishing and its share price was strong (see case study on page 31). Other major companies are similarly running BPR programmes at a time of record profits. The argument is that the best time to conduct such reviews is when an organization is at the peak of its performance and has the resources to invest in it rather than waiting for a serious downturn. Economic and industrial cycles are inevitable. Downturns will surely happen. The companies that will survive them are most likely to be those that are lean and efficient and that have acted proactively to get their house in order before the crisis happens.

By redesigning organizations around their key processes some managerial jobs are inevitably eliminated while others are extended. Those who survive the re-engineering are likely to find themselves with much wider spans of control involving more direct reports and responsibility for areas with which they have little or no familiarity. Functional expertise is no longer a guaranteed route to managerial survival. Skills of managing people, open-mindedness, flexibility and a high-level ability to 'learn while doing' are increasingly important.

(d) Take-overs and mergers

During the economic standstill of the recession, take-over and merger activity slowed down. More recently it has returned with a vengeance. In recent years it has been at fever pitch as major companies around the world have recovered their belief in the advantage of size in the battle for competitiveness. Big is suddenly beautiful again. The result has been bigger and bigger corporations swallowing up smaller firms and merging with organizations that can help to establish their pre-eminence in the market-place. It also means, of course, a lot of rationalization to wipe out duplication of effort and to justify the take-overs. City analysts, wary of the failure of many earlier mergers to deliver on promises of improved performance, are demanding evidence of commitment to cost-cutting before supporting take-over proposals. Greater clarity about cost-cutting goals does not necessarily generate great sensitivity towards clashes of corporate cultures. Cost-cutting and culture clashes threaten managers who thought their careers were secure.

(e) Empowerment

The trend towards empowering non-managerial staff threatens the traditional roles that managers used to perform and erodes their authority. Command and control methods are giving way to coaching and facilitating. Managers are no longer promoted for their technical expertise, but for their ability to manage people, act as a facilitator and serve the needs of their workforce. Managers are now becoming resource providers and diplomats rather than the people at the helm who issue orders and plan strategy. Self-directed teams are increasingly usurping the managers' former roles. For the old-guard managers, brought up on management styles based on command and control, reaching the top is no longer the enticing goal that it used to be. They have become disillusioned, left to brood over what might have been. Former autocratic styles of management are no longer considered appropriate. Many managers are finding the methods in which they have been trained throughout their careers are no longer acceptable, leaving them disoriented and frustrated. The power they anticipated would be theirs when they progressed to the higher reaches of the hierarchy has evaporated before their eyes. They are being urged to give up their old style of management with its emphasis on command and control in favour of less familiar practices of visioning, empowering and coaching. If judged to be ineffective in the new order, these managers risk being forced into early retirement or sidetracked into lower profile jobs.

(f) Job competency profiling

As companies re-engineer their business processes and introduce cultural change they are eager to ensure that the managers they have on board have the right qualities to carry the organization into the future – or that they will be able to adapt to the fundamental changes taking place. This is one of the drivers for job competency profiling that many companies are introducing. Key managers are required to undergo intensive assessments aimed at revealing their job skills and inherent management styles. If these examinations reveal qualities that are at variance with the new corporate culture, the managers concerned have to confront the issue of whether they will be able to fill the gap in their operating styles. Severe mismatches undermine managers' confidence and raise questions about whether they are not so steeped in the old order that they will be unable to adapt to the brave new world. This can have a radical impact on their career plans. For organizations the key issues concern the accuracy and comprehensiveness of the competency profile in relation to the whole range of managerial tasks and the organization's success in assessing each individual manager. For each manager, concerns include the profiling process, the level of organizational support for personal development and the organization's willingness to offer alternative career options.

(g) Outsourcing

Increasingly, major companies are cutting their operations back to their core business and are turning to outside contractors to supply key services that were formerly provided in-house. There is hardly any business function that has not been considered a suitable candidate for outsourcing, ranging from a company's entire computer department, to personnel and corporate relations. As a result entire skill banks are disappearing from companies overnight and being placed in the hands of outside contractors. Managers in these companies who thought they could count on a job for life are suddenly finding that their job no longer exists and the carefully nurtured expertise they have built up devoted to one specialism is no longer a guarantee of advancement. For some, setting up and running their own business to supply services to their former employer is a great opportunity; for others, it is another sign that 'things are not what they used to be'.

(h) Globalization

In the constant drive for efficiency and cost-cutting, many large multinational companies are trying to standardize their operating practices around the world. They whittle down their suppliers to a small handful of those who can comply with their high demands and who can provide the same kind of high standards of service wherever the company operates around the globe – however remotely. Globalization again requires a new breed of manager, one who is at ease operating in different time zones and coping with cultural differences. It is more about being a diplomat and being culturally adaptable than about being a technical expert in any one particular function. The qualities required of the international manager are akin to those of the manager as coach. He or she has to be a facilitator, someone who can handle people – but in this case people with different cultural backgrounds – and there is a need for skills in delegation and monitoring rather than dictatorial issuing of orders. These are skills that often do not come easily to the old-guard generation of managers.

(i) The rise and rise of consultancy

Management consulting firms have not been slow to recognize the opportunities all this turmoil of corporate change has created – indeed some people suggest that quite a bit of it has been generated by the consulting industry. Anxious to benefit from the confusion and disorientation all this rapid change has generated, consulting groups vie with each other to introduce techniques and panaceas that promise to provide the formula that will ensure a smooth passage for companies to their future. Whether it is quality control, BPR, empowerment or open systems, the consulting groups do not lack for ideas when it comes to inventing new ways to solve corporate problems. As each new technique catches on, there is a gold rush in reverse as companies encourage consultants to exploit their riches and to ensure they do not miss out on the new wonder cure. The result is often total upheaval as the companies' operating systems and styles come under the closest of scrutiny and old methods are discredited and replaced by the miracle cure that the leading-edge firms have already shown to be the answer to all those threats to a corporation's survival.

As companies are turned inside out to accommodate the new approach, managers' cosy jobs and career plans are the first casualties. They can forget all the carefully laid plans for reaching the top and the enhanced status they have been striving for all their working life. Someone has shifted the goalposts. The top has become one of those rolling summits that seems to get further away the more you move in its direction. The rules of the game are not what they used to be, and in an empowered organization it is not always clear who is responsible for the supply of a new set of guidelines. You are like an ill-equipped traveller in an uncharted land. Ambitious career plans have to give way to simple survival.

Routes to the top

In a study commissioned by Kinsley Lord, the change management consultancy, David Clutterbuck and Desmond Dearlove concluded that it is no longer possible to plan a career as a logical series of upward moves: 'The rungs on the corporate ladder are vanishing so fast that the concept will soon be redundant altogether. When you think of your career, think not of ladders but of a white-water rapid.'

In truth, added the authors, planning a route to the top never was that easy in Britain. Luck, choice of employer, business discipline, even the school or university you went to, had a part to play. Yet many people learned instinctively the rules of the 'promotion to power' game by following in the footsteps of others. Clutterbuck and Dearlove say that the question today is whether those rules and routes are still valid.

They received an unequivocal answer from Shaun Tyson, professor of human resources at Cranfield School of Management, who told them: 'The traditional model of corporate life has been shattered by the two recessions of the 1980s. Flatter organization structures, large-scale redundancy programmes and the end of any guarantee of a job for life have produced radical changes to the concept of a career.'

Clutterbuck and Dearlove point out that most people have tended to leave career planning to their employer. Those who took the initiative only did so infrequently, at critical points in

9

their life. The authors say that managing a career today is a continuous process for which people have to take responsibility themselves.

Flatter organization structures have reduced promotion opportunities. People in their thirties and forties who have spent their entire careers with one company are now more likely to find themselves stranded on a career plateau or tipped into the icy waters of redundancy than invited into the boardroom.

The authors' research indicates that successful managers will switch employers, sectors and even business disciplines more frequently in future. At the same time it will be increasingly important to notch up certain skills. In many companies, for example, international experience is now almost a prerequisite for senior appointments and many organizations now place a premium on people whose record includes a successful start-up operation or turnaround. Such activities carry a high risk of failure but also attract attention.

The trick today, say Clutterbuck and Dearlove, is to be highly visible at the right time and for the right reasons. Successful operators carefully judge the moment to raise their profile. That means actively seeking to participate in the 'right projects'. Involvement with key projects such as change programmes or human-resource initiatives, for example, can gain people recognition and plug holes in their CVs. Such projects often involve cross-functional teams and have an impact right across the company.

The new career rules, according to Clutterbuck and Dearlove are:

- *Keep an open mind.* You cannot predict where your next big break will come from, so be prepared to switch careers;

- *Take risks – even if they end in failure.* In the new career environment, if you have never failed you have not taken enough risks – but the way you present your failures to the rest of the company is important;

- *Learn to recognize an opportunity.* Do not miss out because it does not come from the direction you expected. Remember, too, that many problems are just opportunities in disguise;

- *Take charge of your career and so reduce stress.* You will have a much better idea of what is going on. If you do not make it to the top, you are in control and can decide to let go if you want to;

- *Remember, there is still time.* Today's flatter organizations mean everyone is closer to the top. Riding the white-water rapid is all about being in the right place at the right time with the right set of skills.

Race to the top

Not everyone is convinced that the obsession with climbing the hierarchy that prevailed before the pyramid became flattened was healthy for companies, or for individual managers for that matter. Michael Blakstad is chief executive of Workhouse, a Winchester-based company which produces television and corporate communications programmes. In the May 1995 issue of *Director* magazine, he questions the conventional wisdom of rewarding a company's star employees by moving them up – and thus away from everything they excelled at. He argues that the time was overdue for finding an alternative to upward advancement.

'Losing your clients' favourite managers to a rival company can be devastating,' he writes. 'However, promoting them to administrative posts inside the organization is seen as good management. The effect can be just as damaging. Important clients become restive at losing their most effective contact, the managers are often unhappy at being taken away from the front line, they aren't always very good at performing jobs they don't enjoy and the company suffers. So why do so many large organizations cut off the hand that their clients most want to shake?'

He adds: 'Let's accept immediately that many of those who transfer to the executive career path are both good at it and prefer to stay there. Provided they have received enough management training, then these are often the best possible people to run the organization. But let's also accept that some of the rain-makers are no better (and possibly worse) at management than specialist administrators and number-crunchers, personnel directors and resource managers. If they have crossed over for the wrong reason, such as status and salary, then both they and the company have lost out.

'This is dawning on a number of Britain's top companies. Their dilemma is how to get their best executives back into contact with clients without the organization falling into chaos. There is no more contentious an issue in management debates. Ambitious men and women resist the idea of recruiting trained administrators to central jobs on the grounds that they cannot possibly know enough about advertising or teaching.

'To get the senior people back to client work represents any number of challenges. That thorniest issue, remuneration, has to be radically revised – many blue-chip companies are keenly aware of the irony in offering people more money to generate less business. Also in need of review are the non-financial means of rewarding success: status, perks, titles and promotion.

'The challenge becomes greater as the star performers get older. An office at headquarters is a more secure place than the long jet-haul or the hotel coffee shop. Commissions from successful accounts are lucrative, but failure could spell a drop in living standards. There are dozens of reasons for clinging to the personalised notepaper and the reserved parking space.'

Employability
In an article in the April 1995 issue of *directions*, the Ashridge journal, the concept of employability is advocated as one solution to the impact of change on career planning. The authors – Laurence Handy, Viki Holton and Peter James, point out in their article, 'Creatures of change', that employees are increasingly bewildered about their future career paths and are demotivated as a result. 'Larger jumps between grades are also making new appointments more nerve-racking for both companies and individuals. Finally, it is becoming more difficult to steer people with high potential through a company in their formative years. These problems can be particularly acute in companies which have decentralized HR responsibilities to their business units.

'The old psychological contract in which managers gave their loyalty in exchange for near-lifetime employment and regular promotions has clearly gone. Its much touted replacement is 'employability', in which employers invest in training and development so that managers can, when necessary, find work elsewhere. The *quid pro quo* is the manager's commitment to the organization for as long as he or she is employed.'

The authors add: 'In the world of employability, responsibility for career development shifts from the organization to the individual. They must now decide their aspirations, define their development needs and be proactive in finding new career opportunities inside and outside their current employer. With fewer promotions, these opportunities will often include horizontal moves as well as developing existing roles.

'The employer's part of the bargain is to provide a substantial infrastructure to support staff. The pioneers, such as Apple and Rank Xerox, are now providing such services as career counselling, career "shops" pulling together details of all corporate vacancies and training and development opportunities and scenarios for future employment trends and skill requirements within the organization. They are making it easier to move between units and functions – by using competency schemes, for example, to highlight similarities between apparently dissimilar jobs, and developing central support to overcome the reluctance of many managers to let good staff go purely for development reasons. They also accept that they must respond to the requests for additional training and development which tend to emerge from such an exercise.'

The authors observe, however, that the attitudes, fears and aspirations of employees are not so easily changed. One company, for example, explained the new world of employability to staff and spent heavily on personal development plans and other initiatives to help them adapt. The employees loved it, but at the end of the exercise many still wanted to know when they would receive their next promotion.

Andrew Mayo, an independent consultant in international human resource management, maintains that employability is more than just being able to get another job if needed. Writing in the October 1995 issue of *directions*, he suggests that 'employability should be the concern of everybody, but it needs to be thought of *internally* as well as externally. A business which has invested in people development cannot wish to encourage the loss of its investment – provided it continues to grow and provide a return. As an individual planning my future, I need to manage my options through developing the skills my organization needs *and* constantly asking the question "what are my saleable capabilities elsewhere?"

'This has important implications for management development. Top-level general management will always be a scarce commodity and, we know, is developed primarily through experience. But "generic" management skills in middle and junior management levels will not be enough to guarantee employability.'

Although the need to be flexible and self-managed is becoming accepted wisdom in today's organizational thinking, Mayo does not hear it much on the lips of the average employee. 'The younger generation has always been adaptable and opportunistic, and this is not news to most of them. But, for those who have put down roots in a particular organization, the concept may be very uncomfortable. Large numbers of people have been through feelings of betrayal, confusion and insecurity, and hope for stability to return.

'The messages people receive are conflicting; organizations tell them that they want more commitment than ever before, *but* don't count on a job for life; work harder with fewer resources *and* take time to look after your own career. Faced with such paradoxes, many people are understandably fearful and totally unprepared. They would much prefer to have a "proper job" with the supporting and social infrastructure that goes with it. The thought of finding customers for themselves is frightening, as is the possibility of irregular income. As a result, in many organizations the old paradigm prevails because people have not been given the time and space to think through the implications of what the new one means.'

The failure by individual managers to adjust to the new realities is probably matched in many cases by an organizational reluctance to face the changes. If the corporate goals are to reduce costs, increase flexibility and adaptability and develop a culture which is much more commercially oriented, then the organization also needs to abandon the old command and control mentality. Loyalty is generated by a two-way process, not the outcome of early personality development. The question facing organizations is whether they want to encourage the belief that managers have a future as well as a present with the organization. If the answer is negative then they need to take a good look at their whole process of human resource management and eliminate everything that would feed any expectation of continuation. If the answer is 'yes', then the next question is 'why?'. If the organization's real aim is to control potentially scarce resources, then a further shift in organizational paradigms is required. Many organizations still think in military metaphors of capturing territories, securing resources, and mobilizing firepower. In a half-century which has repeatedly witnessed the power and success of guerrilla armies, such metaphors are dangerously misleading.

14

The virtual organization

The trend towards the so-called 'virtual organization', which operates primarily through project teams and places high reliance on communications and information technology, is not going to make career planning any easier. Peter Trigg, chairman of Drake Beam Morin (DBM), which claims to be the world's largest outplacement and career counselling organization, observes that: 'In Britain and across the world organizations are reducing their core workforce and making greater use of flexible and part-time workers. Gone are the days of piecework for blue-collar workers. Today, skilled workers at every level are being contracted for project-based work.

'Increasingly many of the new temporary workforces have been victims of redundancy. This experience has broken the psychological bond and trust between employee and employer. Loyalty has died as individuals recognize they cannot look to organizations to provide long-term security.'

Trigg believes that the question of employee commitment must be addressed if organizations are to attract the right individuals for the job. He explains: 'The trend to the "virtual organization" means there will be a much higher proportion of freelance workers and specialists, moving from project to project, employer to employer. The most successful individuals will be those who learn fast, adapt well and embrace new challenges. They will be looking for organizations which offer the opportunity to develop their skills and experience, plus sufficient financial reward. In exchange for which individuals will need to demonstrate commitment to the job – irrespective of the term of the contract.'

One thing seems certain in a very uncertain world – the growth of contract work is sure to continue. While 73 per cent of the British workforce were in permanent jobs back in 1979, only 52.5 per cent are now. Part-time work has risen and self-employment has nearly doubled. The dramatic rise in temporary work has only occurred over the past two years. People used to permanent work will increasingly find themselves on the roller-coaster ride of self-employment or unemployment followed perhaps by a period of contract work, such as interim management.

Roger Young, director general of the Institute of Management (IM), was recently quoted as saying: 'The nine to five job is a thing of the past. Teleworking, home working, outsourcing and interim management are here to stay and set to grow. Flexible employment is now integral to organizational strategy. Employees and employers must learn to adapt and change to ensure future success.'

Young was commenting on a survey into *Long Term Employment Strategies*, published in October 1995 by the IM and Manpower, the leading employment services company. The survey revealed that around 90 per cent of the UK's leading employers use part-time and temporary workers and that 70 per cent contract out non-core operations. It found that all forms of alternative work patterns were set to increase, with over half the respondents predicting an increase in flexible working and contracting out. Four in five employers predicted an increase in flexible working and 70 per cent in contracting out over the following four years.

Cost-cutting was seen by 40 per cent of respondents as the primary factor influencing employment levels. The requirement to increase flexibility, boost productivity and respond to increased competitive pressures were the other key reasons cited.

The survey confirmed the trend away from traditional patterns of full-time core employment towards a wholly flexible employment market. While four in five predicted that 90 per cent of their workforce will remain core employees within the following year, only 47 per cent anticipated this to be the case within a four-year period. Any significant reduction in workforces must be followed by a reduction in the number of managers employed in what have been re-classified as non-core areas.

Despite the apparent end of the recession, restructuring and further job losses were set to continue.

A contract culture?
In a recent television programme Cary Cooper, professor of organizational psychology at the University of Manchester's Institute of Science and Technology (UMIST), pointed out that the phenomenon of contract work was not just confined to Europe. In the US it is known as contingent work. 'I think it is going to move rapidly in this direction as private and public sector companies continue to outsource. My real worry – just in the short and medium term – is that people will feel very insecure because they don't have the skills to cope with contract work; they don't know how to market themselves; they don't know what kind of training they're going to need.

'We have lived in organizations since the industrial revolution. The organizations have managed our careers, they've managed all aspects of our life and the training we've needed. So people are going to have to get the kind of training to make themselves marketable – learn how to market themselves, to play a new set of rules, to develop a new set of attitudes and indeed live with insecurity; because we are entering the age of insecurity. This isn't a small trend. I think we are moving quite rapidly towards a contract culture.'

The insecurity associated with a contract culture will not be confined to individuals. The more that organizations rely on sub-contractors the less capacity they have of their own. This has great advantages in downturns when it reduces break-even levels, but it makes it easier for new market entrants, and it poses threats of being unable to meet customers' demands in upturns. Better planning may not be a realistic answer in the more turbulent environments.

All this insecurity will have a knock-on effect on the economy. People uncertain of their jobs and their futures will be reluctant to invest in new homes or in refurbishing their existing ones – or even in expensive holidays. There is little encouragement to splash out with hard-earned savings when future prospects are so uncertain. Movements, up or down, will be transmitted more rapidly throughout the economy. Larger corporations have, in the past, acted as partial shock absorbers as they have sought to husband resources when faced by downturns.

Suit wars

Those who survive the restructuring and the downsizing may not be as fortunate as at first they seem. Cutting back to core operations inevitably means extra work and long hours for those left behind. The pressure on the survivors – and perhaps the guilt – is more than many can handle. In some cases it has given way to what is becoming known as 'suit wars' – uncharacteristic outbreaks of violence in the changed atmosphere of the workplace.

Professor Cooper of UMIST observes that 'suit wars' are prompted by job cuts and efficiency drives that transform the office environment: 'The people who remain feel more insecure and over-worked. The stress creates a pressure cooker scenario and if you are under pressure, you blow.' Government statistics show that workplace assaults have more than doubled in a decade, creating record violence levels. Some of this may be due to the increased tension caused by the loss of familiar career paths.

Greater control

There will be those who will find it impossible to adapt to the new demands of the virtual organization and who will find project-based work too insecure. They may well find themselves attracted to the idea of becoming teleworkers, operating from home, where they may feel they have greater control over their careers and their future. They might also feel that as free agents they can promote their particular skills in niche markets and map out their careers accordingly, rather than being buffeted and blown off course by the winds of change in corporate life, over which they feel they have little or no control.

Since the trend for corporations is to hone back to their core business and outsource a lot of their former in-house operations, the opportunities to advance as an independent agent are likely to grow at a far greater rate than career opportunities inside corporations. Not everyone is suited to the rigours and disciplines of being a freelance professional or an interim manager, but for many there may be little choice. The changes they will need to make to their operating styles as a freelance are unlikely to be any more radical than the changes that will be imposed on them if they remain as a corporate man or woman.

For organizations the challenge is to find ways to retain their best talent by providing incentives that compensate for job insecurity. The Ashridge Management Index recently concluded that organizations would have to work much harder if they were to retain the loyalty of their senior managers: 'More than half of senior managers feel less loyal to their companies than they did five years ago. Fifty-four per cent are disillusioned about the lack of career opportunities.'

In summary, the problems facing managers and their organizations can be seen as a series of changes that adversely impact on traditional career routes. Such changes include:

- Corporate structural change – flattening of the pyramid, delayering, downsizing, rightsizing.
- Cultural change.
- Outsourcing.
- Empowerment of non-managerial staff.
- BPR – can lead to managers presiding over their own redundancy.
- Job competency profiling – mismatches can result in curtailed careers.

18

- Increasing use of management consultants.

Managers might overcome the adverse impact of these changes on their career paths by:

- Seeking companies that offer employability as a substitute for job security.
- Exploring ways to take responsibility for self-development.
- Developing their own skills at recognizing opportunities, learning rapidly, and coping with the stress of continual development.
- Seeking companies that provide the resources and facilities for self-development.
- Working for smaller companies that may be better training grounds than larger ones for the requirements of the future.
- Seeking companies that build in time to pursue interests not directly linked to the current job brief and that offer the prospects of career progression.
- Considering self-employment – as independent consultants or running their own small businesses.
- Considering becoming interim managers.
- Being less organizationally dependent by teleworking from home.

Chapter Two
Silver Linings in the Clouds of Change

The upheavals in the corporate climate outlined in the previous chapter have had some positive effects for some managers and some organizations in relation to career planning. There are silver linings to the clouds of change. One of the positive outcomes has been to concentrate the minds of managers on the need to conduct regular audits of their careers and to examine how their professional ambitions relate to their life goals. At the same time, organizations have been forced to review their whole approach to career management, to redefine their objectives and their methods. Sadly, the most positive force for bringing this about has probably been the wide-scale managerial redundancies that accompanied the longest recession for many years.

From the perspective of individual managers the older systems and processes of career planning had their drawbacks. In some organizations, career planning was fragmented with well-organized, consistent schemes in parts of the business (e.g. research and development) but little or no structure in other areas (e.g. sales); in others there was a significant formalized system of career planning stretching down several levels of the hierarchy. Such formalized systems frequently constructed career paths in narrow functional silos. Progress to the top was slow, particularly in organizations which were no longer growing. Arrival at the top was often accompanied by a sense of disappointment that the specialization which had been the source of upward movement was now a barrier to further progressions but it was too late to move sideways.

At best, the older systems delivered promotion for most people eventually with, it was hoped, the more able rising faster than their colleagues. The new structures may deliver promotions less often, but if they do arrive, they are to significantly bigger jobs. Seniority and specialization may have become less important as criteria for promotion. For those without specialisms or seniority, that removes constraints. For those who are able, do deliver, learn quickly and are willing to manage their own careers, it creates opportunities.

One of the authors of this book did some consultancy for a large multinational to identify beliefs about and approaches to career management. From a series of interviews at different levels within one function a wide range of individual approaches emerged. Within these individual approaches a number of common features could be discerned. These were brought together in the 'Desert Scene' of self-managed careers:

THE DESERT SCENE OF CAREER MANAGEMENT

PALM TREES   NOMADS

Active Personal
Career Management

Inflexible in
relation to function,
location, etc.

Flexible in relation
to job locations,
etc.

ROCKS

Passive Personal Career
Management

CAMELS

'Palm Trees' were willing to take charge of their careers, develop themselves, look for opportunities but were self-constrained by a chosen inflexibility. They resembled palm trees that stay close to an oasis and put down deep roots. In some cases these roots reflected a strong sense of professionalism that tied them to the function; for others it was an overwhelming preference to remain in a particular location. In any even, their route upwards was very narrow and, when they arrived at the top, it was not necessarily where they wanted to be.

'Rocks' expected the organization to develop their careers for them and saw little or no need to develop themselves in any way. Experience alone was regarded by the Rocks as sufficient grounds for further advancement. (Their progress at the time of the interviews had been very limited.) Underlying the approach and attitude of the Rocks was a level of dependency which was increasingly not being reciprocated by the organization.

'Camels' were willing to adapt but were waiting for the organization to tell them what to do. In the absence of new instructions, they went on doing what they had always done in the apparent belief that their time would come.

In contrast, the 'Nomads' talked about and behaved as if they alone were responsible for their careers. They denied that their careers had ever plateaued because, as they saw it, the moment they found a job no longer developmental they set about finding another one. The Nomads were willing to change function, location, company, etc. as long as the change provided a new job. They created the impression that, because of their approach, all jobs would be found to be developmental by Nomads although they might want to move on sooner rather than later.

When these findings were described to the organization's personnel director he displayed a degree of impatience. When the Nomads were described as behaving as if they had total control over their own careers he broke in angrily: 'That's ridiculous. Even I do not have total control over my career and I am the personnel director.' His own strong sense of professionalism, his attachment to the organization, and, tentatively, the value he appeared to place on his role in the hierarchy was reflected back to him. He thought about this and responded: 'You are saying I have constrained myself.' Despite his obvious success, in comparison to the Nomads, his career had been constrained but not curtailed. Under the older systems of career management he had done well. His unease at this analysis was echoed by many other managers who were unsure how well they would do in the new circumstances.

The other strong impression that emerged from these interviews was that the Nomads, as a group, were the most satisfied with their careers to date. The Nomads' satisfaction was not the product of their effortless rise. Their progress had involved considerable struggle, self-development and career risks and they had not necessarily reached the top. Ruth Tait's recent book, *Roads to the Top*, a study of chief executives, reflects many similar themes. The distinctive characteristic of the Nomads was their complete acceptance of responsibility for their own careers and their refusal to stay with jobs which they no longer found developmental. In contrast, the Rocks were the least satisfied. They had developed at the beginning of their careers and that development appeared to be a one-off. There was little sense of the need for continuing development and a grave reluctance to contemplate any job move which involved risks. The gap between the organization's expectations about careers and those of the Rocks appeared to be widening.

This pattern of varying levels of individual responsibility, active personal career management and flexibility will be found in all organizations at most, if not all, levels. Consulting experience suggests that individuals may move between the four groups in response to events in their private lives, their working lives and the career management policies adopted by their employers. For all groups except the Nomads, an absence of positive intervention by their organizations may result in their sticking to type. Nomads do not reflect a single type but rather a heterogeneous group united by their sense of self-responsibility and their flexibility. For Nomads, the greater freedom which is developing for them to shape their own careers will be met with degrees of delight and awe and simple acceptance. For this group, the more the old formalized approach gives way to more open, integrated systems, the happier they are, because it offers them greater opportunities. They are only too glad to see the back of carefully-tiered succession plans with prescribed entry points and 'experience blocks' that required time served before permitting access to the next level.

The Palm Trees were the major beneficiaries of the older systems. For them the changes represent opportunity and threat simulta-neously. Their familiar 'silo' career path is likely to be much shorter than it used to be – which is a real threat. The greater emphasis on flexibility offers opportunities. To seize those opportunities requires more flexibility than the Palm Trees have exhibited in the past. Palm

Trees have always liked to have some control over their careers and take personal initiatives, but they want to remain part of the organization and will be flexible to achieve this. They lack, to some degree, the self-confidence and self-esteem that enable the Nomads to control their own careers. Camels, without clear guidance from the organization, are likely to experience the changes as a source of real anxiety and frustration. With Camels, the goal for organizations must be to stimulate their sense of self-reliance and control so that they become more actively engaged in managing their own careers.

Rocks might seem unlikely candidates for managerial roles and in well-run organizations they may be very scarce. Elsewhere, they are not uncommon. Managers who signal their reluctance to learn, their impatience with training and development, their belief that their experience gives them all the answers, their unwillingness to coach and develop their own staff, their often unfounded expectation that their organization will recognize their talents and propel them upwards – those are Rocks. In some cases petrifaction appears to be a function of age. In many others it reflects a mind-set. It is the Rocks who find adjustment most difficult if they are made redundant. They expect organizations to deliver them a new career without showing any adaptability or willingness to learn new skills on their part. Such managers are likely to be left on the scrap heap because that is not the way organizations are likely to work in future. Organizations which continue to value experience and seniority but which fail to communicate and fulfil expectations of performance and development are likely to find that their Rock piles are growing larger and more immovable.

New directions

The disappearance of job security has shaken many managers out of their dependency and encouraged them to be more bold in striking out in new directions and taking risks in order to get closer to their career and life goals. Since there is little certainty in today's job market they now feel they do not have a great deal to lose. Managers, who, in more stable times, might have considered discretion to be the better part of valour and decided to stick with a job that appeared to have a secure future, are now released from such constraints. With uncertainty all around them and no guarantee that any job will last, they are obliged to broaden their experience and move around the job market. In many cases, they feel a new lease of life and draw on hitherto untapped inner resources. It has a liberating effect that is good for their careers and probably for their social life as well. They pull themselves out of the rut and enrich their working and private lives. This can only be good for them and for the economy at large.

For many large organizations which used to operate in a command and control style the Desert Scene analysis highlights real threats. Command and control cultures, buttressed by expectations of jobs for life and a commitment to formalized career planning systems, naturally attracted Palm Trees and Camels and did not necessarily dislodge Rocks. It is difficult to imagine they were as successful in attracting and *retaining* Nomads. Faced by increasing competitive pressures organizations need to increase their ratio of Nomads to others if their new structures are to function effectively.

For organizations the new approaches also offer silver linings amid the clouds of managerial redundancies and survivor apprehension. In the past there was what can only be called a fragmented approach to career development in many companies. There may have been an élite of high-flyers who attracted the attention of the HR department, but for most people inside organizations career planning was virtually non-existent. High-flyers attracted disproportionate amounts of time and development costs without necessarily staying to repay the investment. Career planning was tacked on to the appraisal process but many line managers lacked the information and skills to do the job well. The result was confusion, mis-communication and frustration.

In other large companies there was a more formalized approach to developing career paths. Flow diagrams were produced reflecting the impact of qualification and experience in qualifying individuals for the next promotion. Such diagrams, drawn on a functional or sub-functional basis, generated an unnecessary rigidity. If managers completed a certain period of service, obtained a defined set of experiences and qualifications, they were deemed to be candidates for promotion. A candidate for promotion needed to follow certain prescribed routes. These varied between functions, locations and organizations, but they favoured long service and disadvantaged late entrants or those with career breaks. Organizations created what is best described as 'experience blocks' which promotable managers were supposed to move through. The overt rationale was that this would provide career progression and development. A more practical purpose may have been that experience blocks served as rationing devices.

25

In a stable pyramidal hierarchy, promotion opportunities are limited to 'dead men's shoes'. Unless there is an unnaturally high death rate this inevitably means that queues form. Experience blocks generate orderly queues. Paying people to wait in line contributed to the dramatic growth in managerial costs in the 1970s and 1980s. Experience blocks also generate frustration among the more able and ambitious who are reluctant to wait and may, inadvertently, favour the Rocks and the Camels who are prepared to wait until they are called.

In the past the records which were supposed to provide the basis for career development and succession planning were invariably incomplete and out-of-date. The idea that if you were looking for a manager fluent in the Arabic language, with knowledge of the petro-chemical industry and four years' experience of working in a Middle East territory, all you had to do was press a button and out popped half a dozen names, has never been reality. Such systems might have existed for a small élite, but it was never widespread. Ironically the falling cost of information and the growing flexibility of information technology is making it far easier to track large numbers of managers in order to match their skills with the needs of the organization at a time when organizations are busy reducing their managerial stocks.

In the current climate, the formalized approach is too slow and too costly. It assumes that people are going to be around for a lifetime. In the age of short-termism a more focused approach to career development is required. That means organizations need to take periodic snapshots of their managerial talent and decide which people it would be most appropriate to move into constantly changing managerial roles. In such a climate, long-term succession planning would seem to be a dubious investment. Developing and retaining good people is an increasingly vital activity. Attempting to predict strategic leadership needs twenty years ahead is fanciful. For the majority of organizations the focused approach takes them closer to the immediate action. If they do it well they are prepared to do regular audits. Previous conceptions about the managers in the organization may have to be periodically reviewed and perhaps discarded. There is a need to stand back, take a second look at the managerial talent available and to keep an open mind in the light of rapidly changing market forces and their impact on changing priorities for management skills.

The more enlightened organizations are taking this a stage further and are seeking to adopt an integrated approach to career development which tries to match individual aspirations with the needs of the organization. While it would be unrealistic to expect an organization's ongoing needs always to be in tune with its available managerial talent, this is an approach that has much to recommend it. Instead of trying to false-fit managers' skills, styles and aspirations to the market-driven needs of the organization, both requirements are taken into consideration and there is an attempt to arrive at an accommodation that helps to retain the organization's best talent without jeopardizing its future growth.

More and more people are entering the labour market who are better educated, more articulate and very well aware that there is no such thing as a job for life. This inevitably encourages them to be more footloose and more discriminating in terms of their career. Companies realize that if they do not make more effort to meet the needs of such people they will simply walk away – to their competitors. This is more likely to happen as economic recovery takes place and jobs become more widely available. This has injected greater urgency into seeking ways to satisfy the needs of career-resilient managers, which is another positive outcome of the organizational changes sweeping corporate corridors.

Regular audits
A key part of the outplacement programmes companies have put in place to ease the mass exodus is a detailed review of the careers of those managers who have found themselves out in the cold. This in turn has led to the conviction that redundancy is not the only time – or indeed the best time – in a person's career for this important exercise to take place. Regular audits, along the lines of an MOT test, are now being widely advocated by independent career counsellors and those organizations that are taking seriously the radically changed environment for managerial careers. Advocacy by the former might be seen as special pleading; advocacy by the latter is indicative of a real, if unmet, need.

Organizations are seeing the good sense of offering a more methodical approach to career planning as a way to attract and retain talented staff. Managers, for their part, are becoming more selective in the organizations they choose to work for and the extent to which career planning is taken seriously is rapidly becoming one of the key criteria to influence that decision. There are those who believe that career audits conducted by independent counsellors should become one of the perks in a 'cafeteria' of choices offered to managers when discussing salary and benefits packages. Says Judith Mills, director of programmes at London-based Management Career Development: 'One of my dreams is that organizations will allow people to choose the benefits they would prefer and that one of the flexible benefits on offer is a session with a career counsellor. You might not want it every year, but every two years might make sense.'

More say

The new approach means that managers will have a much stronger say in the progress of their career rather than being tied in rigidly to an organization's standardized succession planning process. In other words, managers should be able to enjoy the best of both worlds – greater independence together with the necessary support from their organizations to turn their career ambitions into reality. Electronic aids such as e-mail feedback systems and internal job posting via electronic notice boards should greatly facilitate this 'open market' approach.

If all these concerns are taken on board and organizations and individual managers can find a way forward that it is to their mutual advantage, this can only be a beneficial outcome of all the turmoil created by wholesale structural change. From the organizational point of view, the move away from the cumbersome bureaucracy of the formalized systems can only be welcome. In the past, tracking individual careers was something of a nightmare – an internalization of the planned economy approach with its familiar difficulties of lack of anticipation and misdirection of resources. Today, there are many electronic tools which make it possible to introduce innovative schemes which flag up career opportunities to employees and help senior managers to keep abreast of where the best talent is right now in their organizations. The falling cost of information may have contributed to the destruction of many middle management jobs. On the plus side, it is making possible procedures that could not have been contemplated in the days of paper and card-based systems.

Some managers, looking back on what might appear to them to have been a golden age of stability and reliability, might mourn the loss of more formal career planning systems, even if the perception was often to a large extent an illusion. To retain the loyalty and commitment of such managers, organizations will need to be very clear in communicating what has replaced the old system. While formalized approaches often bypass individual needs in an attempt to be all-embracing, looser more individually-tailored schemes need to be spelled out with clarity or managers will fear that the old system has been abandoned and nothing put in its place. Organizations will need to make a special effort to avoid the escape route of saying that under the new psychological contract individual managers are responsible for their own career progression and fail to provide them with the support, both practical and psychological, for ensuring their future employability

The positive impact of globalization

The trend towards globalization has also had some very positive impacts on career development (see Chapter Ten). While a lot of traditional middle management jobs have disappeared as a result of downsizing, the drive by many companies to internationalize their operations to provide their customers with consistently high standards of service around the globe has created opportunities for career advancement. For those managers with a flair for cross-cultural skills and who are prepared to swap the parochialism of a home-based job for one that requires them to jet around the globe, exciting new vistas have been opened up.

Not everyone is attracted to the idea of long trips away from home and the inevitable disruption to family and social life, but far from blocking career progression, globalization promises to be one of the liberating factors that can bring a new lease of life to managers who might have hitherto found themselves in something of a parochial rut.

At 3M, for example, a major delayering exercise has reduced the number of rungs in the UK organization's promotional ladder. However, the restructuring has coincided with a move towards globalization. Managers in 3M's UK organization are finding fewer opportunities for advancement within the local company, but challenging new opportunities are emerging on the international front for those with the skills and the motivation to take advantage of them.

City-based Standard Chartered Bank is going in virtually the opposite direction (see Chapter Ten). It has whittled down its expatriate cadre from around 800 to 160 people in favour of opening up more senior jobs to local nationals. The change of policy is driven by cost constraints and the trend towards indigenization in many of the countries in which the bank has operations. At the same time, however, the route to the top posts in the bank, which used to be almost exclusively via long service and broad expatriate experience, is now being thrown open to people with specialist skills in the areas the bank sees as providing the greatest opportunities for growth.

In both 3M and Standard Chartered Bank, it is not so much a case of opportunities for advancement disappearing but of new routes to the top opening up. It means that in order to advance, managers in both companies need to keep abreast of the new trends and adapt their development plans accordingly. It also means keeping their ear to the network to be constantly updated on where specifically new opportunities are emerging and to ensure they maintain a high enough profile to be considered as candidates for the jobs that are going to be key to the company's thrust into the future.

A more fruitful career

Taking a positive view, there are some clear advantages in the changed order for organizations. If managers' expectations shift so that they no longer think in terms of long-term employment, there is likely to be more flexibility in the workforce and it could serve to encourage organizations and employees to focus more sharply on what constitutes a satisfying and fruitful career. If organizations successfully manage to develop a fully-integrated approach to career planning, there is the potential for achieving a highly motivated and efficient workforce. Although no two individuals are likely to share precisely the same aspirations, a greater awareness of what each is seeking can help organizations to fine-tune their career development programmes. Inevitably, there will be some managers whose abilities and aspirations do not match the requirements of the organization. Incumbents who find themselves in this position will have to look elsewhere. Ultimately, the organization will attract the kind of managers that best suit its needs and culture.

Japanese car companies, for example, put a lot of effort into recruiting people who appear to be in sympathy with the organization's values, which broadly involve teamwork, co-operation, quality of work etc. People who are at home in such a culture are attracted to work at such firms. There are other, perhaps more sales-focused organizations that value such qualities as achievement, performance and initiative. From time to time, companies adapt their cultures to the needs of the day, but in general they create a working climate they are comfortable with and hire the kind of people who work well in such climates. The integrated approach to career planning provides the opportunity for both the organization and the individual to examine to what extent their needs are matched and should, if followed through properly, lead to an organization of switched-on employees.

CASE STUDY: Shell International

Many companies have seen the turbulent changes in the economic climate as an opportunity to review their business processes and to streamline their structures, resulting in leaner and fitter organizations. Some have rationalized just as business is beginning to look up and the bad times seem to be behind them. They have stuck to their guns, however, despite some criticism, arguing that economic downturns will always be lurking over the horizon and that the best time to restructure is during an upturn when there are the resources available to make a good job of it. Proactive action is always better than ill-timed reaction to crisis.

Shell International, for example, streamlined its central office and support services at the beginning of 1996, reducing staff from around 7,000 to 5,500 at a time when trading seemed to be on an upswing. The reduction was the result of a policy to simplify central office and support functions and to devolve more responsibility for career planning and performance appraisal to line management and to individual managers. At the same time, it was decided to place more emphasis on current performance than on potential when evaluating managers' careers, although at the more senior levels Shell still puts much store on potential. If it fails to give due attention to those who are likely to be running the company in future it would, of course, soon be in trouble, but at the levels below senior management it recognizes that rapid change makes it virtually impossible to predict which jobs will be of greatest value more than a few years down the line.

The reduction of staff in the latest reorganization may seem dramatic at first sight, but in the context of a total workforce of 100,000 worldwide it is hardly a radical cutback. However, it is the latest episode of an irrevocable process that has seen Shell's workforce

31

halved in the past thirty years. George Lefroy, head of senior management resourcing at Shell's head office in London recalls:

'In almost every one of my twenty-nine years at Shell there has been a reduction in the size of the workforce. It's been mostly a series of steps, sometimes fairly dramatic steps, sometimes a bit of marking time, sometimes even creeping upwards in number, but it's been a long duration. Some of that has been Shell recognizing that certain activities that we've done traditionally are far better done by contractors or independent agents. At one extreme there was the whole business of service station operations and supply of the product in lorries to the countryside. Typically, if you go back thirty years we owned and managed the service stations with Shell staff, we delivered every last drop of fuel with Shell drivers in Shell tankers to every last village.

'We quickly saw that there were some of those activities where we didn't have a competitive edge at all, where contractors or independent businessmen could do a far better job. So typically we withdrew from involvement in many of those activities.'

Similarly, Shell concluded that many aspects of prospecting for oil and designing and constructing offshore oil platforms could better be sub-contracted to specialists. In recent years, it has become obvious that such activities are not core to Shell. As Lefroy explains, Shell now focuses on a much narrower band of core activities: 'We are an integrated energy company and we are also the world's largest petro-chemical company. That's where our core business is and we want to position ourselves with investments and operations such that we can run those businesses either directly or perhaps indirectly through joint ventures in certain countries where we need local partners or other international companies as partners. So we have been gradually in staffing terms shedding those activities which are not core and coming back to those activities that are core, and the 100,000 people we now have in Shell run a very much larger business than the 200,000 people we had when I joined the company. Of course, our 100,000 people probably manage three-quarters of a million other people via the contractors, agents and distributors and so on who are in effect conducting an element of our business for us.'

The latest reorganization of Shell's central office has also attempted to devolve responsibilities and simplify procedures: 'We have tried to simplify our service companies and clearly distinguish the roles which are service providers from the roles that are shareholder responsibilities. In the old organization that was rather hard to determine because almost everyone had an element of both hats. Again this is a process that has been going on for a long time and the latest review is just accelerating that process.'

While eager to simplify its processes, Shell needs to maintain cohesion between its many operations scattered around the world. It had to decide which were the activities that it was important for the central organization to retain and which it could devolve to line management: 'What matters very much to us centrally as a group is the development of senior management and the recruitment of people who might come through to senior management. The whole senior management cadre is one of the very important means by which we bring cohesion to this group, because we are very decentralized. We want to maintain all the benefits of decentralization while having the benefits of being one of the largest international groups in the world.

'You must choose what you are going to manage because when you have four or five group managing directors as we have in our new organization and only 140 people in the corporate centre supporting those four people, you need to rethink your processes.'

As part of the reorganization Shell re-examined the way it manages its human resources and the HR department's relationship between the centre and those running its international businesses. The result was a very different organization to the one it had before. Lefroy says: 'There are seventeen of us in HR at the corporate centre for this large group, which ultimately manages three-quarters of a million people indirectly and 100,000 directly. Management development is an absolutely critical success factor for the Shell group. It always has been and always will be in the future.'

A re-examination of the HR function led to a profound debate around the whole question of the employer/employee psychological contract: 'I don't think we've ever promised lifetime employment, but there's no doubt that most of our people *believe* they have been promised lifetime employment by the company despite going through exercise after exercise in which they watched their colleagues leave.

'Of course the reality is that no one has a contract for life in Shell and no one ever has had a contract for life, although there are all sorts of processes that keep people in jobs, in some cases even while under-performing. So we have the concept of the psychological contract and the question for us was: are we changing it so dramatically now? My answer is we are not changing it very dramatically, but there was a perception in some people's minds that we were and therefore many things have to change, such as the way we go about managing people.'

In the past Shell has always regarded managers' potential as an important element of performance appraisal, but recent trends have placed more emphasis on current performance. All business change points in that direction at the moment. There is much more focus on the bottom line and on the return to shareholders; on delivering the product; on setting stretch targets and achieving those apparently unachievable targets. It was obvious to Shell, in the light of this trend, that it needed a much stronger performance culture. It therefore had to ask itself some further questions: if performance management is going to become more prominent, what is the relevance of potential for Shell? Is it something that should continue to have currency or not?

George Lefroy says: 'At the end of the day we have said that potential is still very important to us because we still want to develop top management for the long haul. We are still in business for the long haul. We still typically build very large projects that take five years in the design phase, five years in the construction phase and run for ten to thirty years. So we are not the kind of company that is in and out of things every five minutes. Of course we have to be nimble, but many of the things we are doing are inherently long term. So we must still have that very long-term view even though we don't promise lifetime employment to everyone. What we do promise is that the good performers, in situations where the business allows it, have got a prospect of very long-term employment, if not a lifetime.'

Not every employee wants a job for life. Shell has identified different aspirations among different categories of managers working for it: 'It's fashionable for young people today to talk about job-hopping careers, jumping from job to job. We see more evidence of that in our financial and commercial people than we do in technical people. Technical people, provided we are challenging them, will expect there to be a good and interesting job in Shell. Financial and commercial people are much more attuned to the outside world – very much more alert to all the things that might be going on out there. So we tend to have a higher turnover of them than we had ten or twenty years ago.

'The other element is the specialist where the specialism is not core to us. In those areas we may very well be satisfied with moving people in and out of jobs and accepting that individuals will also want to move in and out of jobs. There are one or two jobs where we deliberately go for an outsider. Our chief economist is invariably an outsider who comes in on a three-year contract and goes on to do something else afterwards. The reason is we actually want someone who won't look at things through Shell eyes and will help us to look at the economic world out there in a different way.'

The changes in the market-place encouraged Shell to look more closely at the balance between measuring performance and potential. It concluded that potential was still very important. It was highly valuable in helping to judge who in a particular country should be developed for a senior management post or in picking someone to be seconded to a particular country. Such people need more than professional expertise. They need additional qualities that will help them to cope with different cultures. Lefroy adds: 'So there's no question of abandoning potential; it's a matter of changing the balance somewhat between the measurement of performance and the measurement of potential. Much more energy now goes into the management of performance and the measurement of it and less energy into the measurement and management of potential.'

This has led to a change in the balance of control between the centre of Shell and its operating units. The Corporate Centre will now only be involved in the measurement of the potential of the most senior managers in the group. For them it has a prescribed methodology for measuring potential which it requires the operating units to apply and then feed back the relevant information to the centre. As far as the rest of the workforce is concerned, the centre has devolved responsibility to the operating units. They are free to use the prescribed system of measurement or not. It is their decision. Even if they apply the same measurement techniques for all levels of staff, Shell's central office HR department will not be part of the process of evaluating the results. It will only play an active role in the development of high-potential managers who might ultimately reach the upper echelons of the organization.

The main instrument for career planning and development in Shell is now what is known as the *current appraisal summary* (CAS), which is completed by the individual in conjunction with his or her line manager and HR manager. Parts of it are updated annually, other parts every two years. In line with the aim for more open processes at Shell and for staff to take more responsibility for their own development, ownership and responsibility for the CAS's status rests with the individual. The individual can access CAS electronically and can input new information at any time in the section that deals with 'own wishes and views'. This is broken down into general comments, development direction and mobility. Lefroy says:

'It is very important for us to know his or her wishes and views because we move people around and you generally find people's mobility changes with different stages of their professional life. Typically, when they're young they are more mobile; then they get to a certain point – probably in their forties – when their children are starting at secondary school and they become rather immobile. In their fifties they may become more mobile again. Their children are through secondary school and they are then able to move.'

The individual might also be concerned about breadth of experience, not just geographic mobility, to ensure employability. Individuals might identify a particular area in which they would prefer to work. They might, for example, record that they would like to make a move towards general management to gain broader experience, rather than climbing a narrow professional ladder. They might say the reverse. They might have tried a spell in general management, not found it to their taste, and record that they have decided that they are more comfortable being a project engineer, for example, and would like to specialize and become more expert in that specific area.

Other parts of the CAS record 'performance narrative', a brief description of the individual's job and his or her potential, which is reviewed every two years. Both job description and potential are agreed with the person's line manager. Under 'current assignment history', details of key results/experience, competence acquired and training received are recorded. Finally there is a section dealing with career planning, which is completed with the individual's HR manager and line manager. This includes a 'pen picture' which is a summary of around forty words describing the individual as a person. Development needs, possible next jobs and longer-term career plans are also recorded in this part of the CAS.

The new approach to career planning was introduced at Shell at the beginning of January 1996, initially at top management levels, and is gradually being cascaded down to the rest of the organization.

Some companies have separated performance appraisal from career planning so that managers feel less constrained in setting out their career ambitions, but Shell has decided that the two areas are interdependent. Performance assessment will remain an annual requirement for all Shell staff, involving prior discussion and the setting of performance targets and subsequent reporting and discussion of achievement against them. It incorporates concepts such as 360-degree appraisal and self-appraisal, with an emphasis on results rather than effort. It will normally be coupled with annual ranking of performance. Operating companies and units are free to design their own systems but a best practice guide has been developed for them.

As part of the greater emphasis on current performance Shell has introduced variable salary packages for senior managers that are linked to the performance of the individual and the company and team he or she works for. Although Shell has no plans to give greater rewards to managers who are prepared to move laterally, the aim is to provide more flexibility in the remuneration system and to give more scope for people to move about in it. Shell makes it clear, however, that the rate at which people can expect to move within the new system is directly related to their work performance.

There are a number of new elements. Stock options are now available to the top 1,000 managers at Shell, whereas in the past it was confined to the top 100. In this case, of course, the benefits are directly linked to how well Shell as a group performs on the stock market. Senior managers can also earn bonuses according to how closely their operating companies perform to plan during the financial year. Another bonus is linked to individual performance measured against the peer group.

The key principles underlying all the changes in Shell's career development programme are:

- Emphasis on performance management.
- Simplification of processes to improve understanding to ensure that they can be used with the minimum of staff support.
- Increased ownership by, and involvement of, individuals and line managers in debates about competencies, performance and prospects.
- Openness and transparency.

37

Chapter Three
Prospects for Women Managers

The trend towards 'softer' management styles, using coaching and facilitating rather than autocratic approaches, is widely predicted to favour women managers, but research by Kingston Business School indicates that the wholesale restructuring organizations have been undergoing in recent years, particularly where downsizing and delayering are involved, has had mixed blessings for women managers.

The proportion of top British companies with women directors nearly doubled – from 8 per cent to 15 per cent – during 1995, according to a survey by Opportunity 2000, the equal opportunities lobby. It represented women's biggest advance into company boardrooms since the 1975 Equal Opportunities Act. The number of women in senior management posts has not kept pace. A 1995 survey by the Institute of Management found that, in a sample of 300 companies, the number of women managers had risen in the previous twelve months from 9.5 per cent to 10.7 per cent, but predictions were that the figure would rise to 20 per cent across the private and public sectors.

Lady Howe, Opportunity 2000's chairwoman, maintains that after twenty years women are making their presence felt at all levels of management: 'There is still a very clubby, male culture in business, but gradually this is changing.'

Senior women managers are still to be found principally in fields such as personnel and marketing, rather than research and development, manufacturing and production, but their march to power extends across all businesses, from the giants of the FT-SE 100 index to small private firms.

Liz Bargh, Opportunity 2000's director, believes some people might be tempted to see the number of companies that have joined Opportunity 2000 and the resulting promotion of female staff as a manifestation of 'political correctness'. In fact, she maintains, the trend has been driven by 'economic imperatives rather than altruistic or public-pressure considerations. This is not just about social or perceived social justice. We believe these companies see it as enlightened self-interest. Many companies, such as banks and retailers, are realizing that with females making up more than half their customers and workforce, these issues have to be addressed.'

The upturn in the fortunes of women managers in the UK is a very new phenomenon. As recently as 1994 an Institute of Management survey revealed a decline in the proportion of women managers at almost all levels of management and noted that women were twice as likely to resign in a period of downsizing. Professor Christine Edwards, head of the School of Human Resource Management at Kingston Business School, cautions that it would be unwise to read too much into the latest statistics. She points out that the Opportunity 2000 findings are based only on companies that are committed to setting targets to progress women's careers and may not be representative of the corporate community at large. Similarly, the Institute of Management surveys only relate to IM members. Professor Edwards observes:

'However, it is probably about the best information we have because if you look at crude statistics it is very difficult to classify what a manager is. But if you just take people who are in higher grades in organizations, there's no doubt that women are very under-represented in organizations as a whole. Women have always been a minority in the labour force, particularly in positions of responsibility and that's even been true in sectors that employ mostly women.'

She notes a plus side to the downsizing trend, however: 'Many downsized companies have curtailed external recruitment and strengthened their commitment to management development in order to exploit their existing talent. At least one survey has found that women can benefit from such "grow your own" policies. Increased dependence upon an internal market could, *ceteris paribus*, advantage women candidates.'

Professor Edwards maintains that a more significant labour market trend reflects factors which changed the demand for particular kinds of managerial or professional expertise. Most notable of these, she says, is a reorientation of companies towards the needs of internal and external customers in response to the increasing competitive environment for private companies and a government-led imperative for those in the public sector. She adds: 'Where the customer base consists of a large proportion of women, or where women are thought to possess the kind of interpersonal skills needed to relate to customers, then women managers may find advancement easier. Allied to this "cult of the customer" is the expansion of a number of specialisms – customer relations, advertising and marketing – where women are better represented. Growth in management posts in these areas, therefore, is likely to increase the number of women in management.

'A further major feature of management in the 1980s has been the emphasis on the management of human resources within organizations and growth in employment in the personnel function. Personnel is another specialism with high numbers of women managers.'

The combined effect of decentralization and delayering on middle management roles has brought a shift from technical to general skills and an emphasis on managing people. Successful managers today need to replace the command and control management style associated with the traditional, large-scale bureaucracy and adopt that of coach, counsellor, team leader and facilitator. 'A move away from technical expertise to a general one based on a more people-centred approach would appear at first sight to benefit women. Some writers, for example, maintain that women are more concerned with relationships and have better interpersonal skills than men. However, it is uncertain how far managerial selection is made on the basis of these "new" characteristics or whether women have better interpersonal skills.'

Professor Edwards points out that some research suggests that managers are still promoted on the basis of 'individualistic, competitive and assertive behaviour'. She questions whether in fact managerial styles have actually changed all that much: 'There are two sorts of information on this. There's the guru-type literature and the consultant-inspired type literature which says: This is how it ought to be. Then there is the hard research which has tried to evaluate what has actually happened. In terms of the latter, we don't have a great deal of information of what is actually happening in organizations. Certainly at one of the organizations I was looking at there was a lot of talk about changing people's managerial styles, changing the core competencies that were required to carry out managerial roles, but we aren't too sure what is happening in reality.

'There are also a lot of countervailing factors like, for example, performance-related pay, which is actually part of a much more macho tradition of management. The theory behind it, that people are much more motivated by money, that you reward the winners and the performers is very individualistic. Those sorts of systems are being introduced in organizations that are talking about teams!'

The HR department of a public service utility that Christine Edwards studied was trying to introduce managerial competencies as a way of pinning down what would be required of new managerial roles. 'What they were doing was actually looking at the jobs that were there and deriving competencies and personal specifications from incumbents, which were the old-guard men. In fact one of the most highly-promoted women, who by virtue of the sponsorship of the chief executive had got a position at the time of the structural change, said to me: "I would never get my job now, because the competencies now attached to it relate to qualities and skills I don't have."'

In Professor Edwards' experience, it is difficult for organizations to change the *status quo* unless they go to the expense of recruiting extensively from outside. Traditionally, promotions into senior management have been from pools of male-dominated middle managers and administrative staff. Even though these are the areas of management which have been hit most hard by downsizing exercises, old traditions die hard. It is demotivating to ignore the survivors and to recruit from the external market at a time when an organization is trying to recover from the shell shock of delayering. At the same time organizations have to consider whether the newly-defined competencies that they may have to go outside to find are more important than an intimate knowledge of the business and specialist technical expertise built up over years of service. In some organizations, like pharmaceutical companies, ongoing expertise is critical.

Professor Edwards points out that there are in any case other ways to acquire the so-called 'soft skills' without increasing the proportion of women in an organization: 'One of the responses to the need for counselling, team-building and interpersonal skills is not necessarily to recruit a woman, but to put a man on a course, which is much cheaper and easier if you've got a lot of men in place.'

A typical feature of the traditional large-scale bureaucracy was a division between line and staff management. In the past these represented two distinct career paths for managers – general managers who moved between line and staff in a spiral or a 'Y' form in order to progress their careers, and support staff who advanced within their own specialism. Christine Edwards says: 'Women have traditionally made their careers in support functions rather than through the line and advancement through these specialist "functional chimneys" may be threatened by organizational restructuring. However, restructuring has also significantly changed career paths for general management. In the large-scale, multi-layered organization, the general managers gained experience by spiralling around the organization through relatively fast and frequent promotions. The path to senior management in particular usually entailed geographical mobility, continuity of service and substantial experience of the central function. All these factors put women, especially those with partners and families, at a disadvantage.

'In flattened organizations middle management roles have become wider and there is often an increased use of project teams. This implies that the broad experience gained by spiralling could now be gathered without recourse to changing jobs and location. Moreover, with the break-up of large central corporate departments and devolution of responsibilities to middle management, it could be argued that the kind of responsibilities and status formerly associated with senior management are now relocated in the middle levels of the organization.

'Thus it could be that future women managers may be content to remain where they are and the significance of the glass ceiling will be diminished.'

Professor Edwards adds, however, that devolution may have its disadvantages. Increased workload and longer hours are often the outcome of the devolution of responsibilities to middle management, factors which are said to deter women with families from seeking management posts. Moreover, there is increased competition for the senior management jobs that remain.

This view is supported by research undertaken by the Institute of Management which found that women in top jobs are much less likely than their male colleagues to be married or have children.

A study of 1,500 members of the institute found that one third of the women managers were unmarried, compared with only 8 per cent of men. When they did marry, the women were more likely to divorce or separate; 12 per cent of women and 5 per cent of men were divorced or separated. Only 49 per cent of women in the study had children, compared with 86 per cent of men. This provides further evidence that the advance of women to the boardroom and management suite can only be achieved by sacrificing their personal lives.

At one major company that Professor Edwards studied she identified three serious setbacks to women's careers. One was that, at a time of economic stringency and fierce competition, the company placed emphasis on selling rather than marketing, an area where women are generally considered to excel. Secondly, the marketing department, which used to be organized on a country by country basis, expanded its role to cover the whole of Europe. This meant that unless they were prepared to go and live in Brussels or to spend half their life in an aeroplane, the opportunities for women to progress in the marketing department were severely limited. Thirdly, much of the central HR function was devolved to line managers, again resulting in a decline in the number of opportunities that favour women's skills.

Management development opportunities
Changes in managerial responsibilities, role and style, Professor Edwards argues, suggest a central place for management development in any organizational strategy for change. 'Career planning also has greater significance in the absence of clearly defined career paths. Furthermore, it could be argued that access to appropriate management development opportunities and career advice may be critical to long-term employment, let alone career advancement, in the more competitive environment of the 1990s.'

There is considerable evidence, claims Professor Edwards, that women lose out on access to formal training opportunities: 'Access to organizationally sponsored training and development schemes and to education opportunities is unequal and while women are not under-represented at the start of graduate trainee "fast tracks", they are likely to "leak out" as they receive assignments further away from the core business. Fast tracks are also exclusionary for those women who are late entrants to management. Generally, it seems that women are less likely to benefit from formal processes of management development than men. However, most management development is achieved through work experience and it may be that access to a variety of work assignments is more significant for career progression than formal training.'

CASE STUDY: A public service utility

A study by the Kingston Business School of the impact of structural change at a public service utility (PSU) has thrown some interesting light on future career prospects for women managers. The investigation showed that the growth in management jobs, combined with a process of breaking up existing organization power structures and career paths, opened up some opportunities for women. A reduction in emphasis on length of service and engineering experience as criteria for entry into management, and changing definitions of the skills and expertise required for managerial roles, were significant factors in this process. In particular, the relegation of the previously dominant engineering department to a servicing role destroyed its monopoly of the main paths into key management posts.

Restructuring at the PSU also brought significant changes in managerial roles and the skills and experience needed to fill them. A loosening of the technical requirements for general management and the inclusion of business and 'people management' skills allowed some women to enter these posts in the initial restructuring period. Sponsorship by the chief executive and other senior managers also assisted a very small number of women into key senior positions formerly exclusively occupied by men.

Despite some gains, the analysis also shows that women's advancement, especially at middle management levels, was severely limited. It was more modest than the expansion of women in the workforce as a whole, suggesting that feminization alone does not necessarily lead to a proportionate growth in women managers.

Professor Edwards says: 'Not only was the increase in numbers small, but women had largely failed to establish themselves in the line management posts central to the organization. This is partly because there were very few women employed in these central areas and expansion in management was for the most part the result of upgrading existing staff. However, our case shows that the operation of a strong labour market in a male dominated organization, excludes the possibility of remedying the gender imbalance through external recruitment.

'Women have typically made their careers in the support functions of organizations, often using professional qualifications as a means to progression. A significant finding of the research therefore was the failure of women to capitalize on expansion in the professional specialisms, notably personnel, in which they were most strongly represented. This is directly attributable, at least in part, to the process of decentralization which devolved significant corporate responsibilities to the local level. Decentralization of the central support functions, most notably personnel, to the business units resulted in a demand for a broader range of skills and general management experience than that normally held by women who had followed highly specialized and narrowly-focused careers in the organization.'

An additional factor stemming from devolution at the PSU was the long hours and pressure of work experienced by senior and middle management. This made these posts unattractive to men and women with family commitments. While unsocial hours and work overload has always been a feature of general managers' posts, its extension to the support functions is likely to prove a deterrent to some women seeking promotion or joining the organization in the future.

Despite significant changes in career paths, neither men nor women working at the PSU had received significant assistance with their career planning and development. Delayering and devolution had resulted in changes to both specialist and general management roles and broad organizational experience was found to be essential to career success. However, access to the key developmental experiences – lateral moves, projects and secondment – was gained through sponsorship, networking and 'being visible': processes where women have been shown to fare badly.

Professor Edwards concludes: 'Writers on women managers often propose management development, career planning and equal opportunities practice as the primary means by which employers can assist women in their careers. Our research suggests that such remedies are unlikely to have much effect in the face of the major barriers posed by much of the organizational change that we have examined.'

Chapter Four
The Quest for Leadership

One feature of the consulting work carried out by one of the authors of this book has been the upsurge of interest by clients in leadership and change. Organizations are increasingly recognizing the need for more leadership and better change agent skills as they seek to respond to the competitive pressures that threaten them. Yet, in working with clients, a number of apparent paradoxes have become increasingly evident.

The press is full of articles about the enormous salaries top directors receive. The average top executive's salary in the UK is now reckoned to be twelve times that of the average worker's earnings. Ten years ago it was only eight times greater. There is a lot of evidence to show that the disparity of earnings between the top and bottom of the hierarchy is widening and managerial salaries have risen significantly in real terms in the 1980s and 1990s. The gap grows the higher up the hierarchy you go. At the same time, however, organizations are delayering. They are cutting out huge swathes of managers. There must be more unemployed managers today than there have ever been. There have never been so many former executives offering themselves as consultants of all sorts, interim managers, and part-time managers. From an economist's perspective this represents something of a paradox. How can it be that there is such an excess of redundant managers at a time when executives' relative earnings are rising? Conventional economic theory suggests that excess supply of any product or service tends to lower its price. Given the extent of job losses and the ready availability of formerly employed managers and executives there is a case for arguing that there is oversupply in the market for managers and yet the price of managers, as reflected in their real earnings, their perks, their pensions and their status symbols has continued to rise. How can this be?

The pressures to reduce managerial numbers became very evident in the recession of the early 1990s. Job cuts by organizations were a predictable response to trends which had existed for the best part of this century and which had begun to threaten firms' competitiveness. In the past we have seen an explosion in the number of managers as organizations prospered and expanded. According to one estimate, the number of managers in the UK tripled to over two million between 1911 and 1971 – and the number of managers continued to grow. Organizations that had previously largely eschewed the benefits of professional management (e.g. the National Health Service) began to draw lessons and practices from the private sector. At the same time the growth of information-related jobs held by highly qualified individuals led to an increased use of managerial titles and job grades for staff who lacked any direct reports.

The growth in the number of managers relative to other groups naturally increased the proportion of total costs attributable to overheads. This trend was accelerated in the 1980s by the increase in the real earnings of managers and those on managerial grades. In some organizations the impact on overheads of these two trends was sufficient to reduce reported profits significantly. It also provided scope, in a number of widely reported takeovers such as that by Hanson of BAT, for quick cost reductions and profit improvements by slashing head office numbers. If the recession of the early 1980s saw dramatic changes in working practices and staffing levels on the shopfloor, the early 1990s recession saw that policy transferred to other levels of the hierarchy. Organizations were finding managers as a group increasingly expensive because of their growth in numbers and the widening gap in the dispersion of earnings.

Alarmed by rising levels of overheads and the need to cut costs in the face of a very severe recession, organizations questioned the value of having so many managers. Once asked, that question prompted speculation about the organizational benefits of having fewer managers. Fewer managers would result in shorter lines of communication, quicker decision-making, less bureaucracy, more scope for individuals to use their initiative and abilities. Organizations, in turn, would become more cost-competitive, more flexible, more responsive, more focused. Reducing the numbers of managers would have real benefits to the organizations concerned, provided that the managers who remained could cope with their escalating responsibilities.

The paradox of rising pay

The need to reduce costs explains the oversupply of managers or ex-managers. How to account for the continued rise in real incomes even when organizations are making managers redundant? That explanation revolves around the nature of managerial work and the skills it requires. Working with managers in the UK and elsewhere, one of the authors always asks: 'In what circumstances do organizations need managers?' The repeated and consistent answer has been that managers are needed to produce stability, order and efficiency. Managers are needed when an organization wants people who are really good at repeating the existing theory of business, the currently known rules of business success, people who are good at honing and improving the current recipe. Organizations were hiring more and more people who were good at, and were encouraged to be good at, managing stability or, at best, slow change. Asking the same groups of managers the question: 'In what circumstances do organizations need leaders?' also produced remarkably consistent results. Leaders are required at times of change, in periods of transformation, when new theories of business must be developed.

The needs of organizations are shifting. Organizations are facing greater demands for change than before because of intensifying global pressures. If the pace of change continues to rise – and it shows little or no sign of slowing down – the demand for leaders is likely to rise dramatically. At the same time, the changes that have taken place inside organizations have also increased the demand for leadership skills and behaviour: one obvious consequence of delayering organizations is that the span of control rises. Having more direct reports and a bigger job in times of increasing change requires high-order leadership skills. Organizations need fewer managers, but more leaders.

Organizations are trying to be more selective about the people they hire and promote. When they advertise for people who are entrepreneurial, risk-taking, visionary, interpersonally skilled, cross-culturally sensitive, self-reliant, cognitively focused, they are advertising for leaders. Leaders are not required just at the top of organizations but at all levels of the hierarchy. Relying on leadership just at the top ignores the need for greater flexibility and responsiveness at all levels.

More leaders, fewer managers

If this is what is happening, then one possible explanation of the paradox is that organizations are seeking to hire and retain more leaders and fewer managers. Companies used to be prepared to hire managers and hope that a reasonable proportion of them would turn out to be leaders. They are increasingly confronted by the fact that today they need to hire and promote people who already display leadership skills – not just at the top of the organization, but at all levels, particularly as they decentralize. The reward structures and systems that were originally designed to attract and retain managers are increasingly being used to attract and retain leaders. One interesting tacit assumption of this approach is that leaders have the same values and respond to the same rewards as managers. Given the potential differences in style and orientation towards change between the two groups, this seems a highly questionable assumption.

Traditionally, managers became managers because they were good at what they did and they had appropriate qualifications and experience. The experience related to the job they were already doing, not to their new managerial role. In addition, in the old hierarchies, with their single pay spines, people were given managerial titles and grades to reward and retain them. There were managers who did not manage anybody. They were not necessarily any good at managing people, but they were paid as managers. Becoming a manager in these circumstances was not particularly difficult, provided one was appropriately qualified and, with the expansion of higher education, there were more and more qualified people available. In order to make anyone a manager all the organization needs to do is give that person the authority necessary to do the job. The individual may not be a very good manager but their authority will see them through most difficulties. Long-term data for over half a century in Britain revealed a relative decline in managerial rewards which suggests that, overall, supply was more than equal to demand. Such an outcome is entirely consistent with the growth of higher education in Britain.

Unfortunately organizations cannot make people into leaders. Only those who are prepared to follow can determine who is a leader. Qualifications may help, authority has its advantages but, ultimately, leadership rests on the consent and trust of the led. Without that trust and consent there is no leadership. In an ideal world all managers would possess excellent leadership skills. In the real world many of those whose people skills might kindly be described as rudimentary and whose change management skills were, at best, underdeveloped, were appointed to managerial positions.

A double disadvantage

If organizations cannot, by the grant of authority, make people into leaders, they need to become much smarter at identifying, recruiting, developing and retaining leaders. If leaders are possessed of skills and attributes less widely distributed than the persistence and intelligence needed to gain qualifications and become a manager, then appointing lots of people to managerial positions has the double disadvantage of being expensive and unlikely to succeed. Recruiting people perceived to be successful leaders in other organizations is no guarantee of success. Many such recruits prove to be incapable of engendering the same response in the new setting and are replaced.

Are leaders more scarce, less readily available than managers? We believe that they are and that a number of interesting recent organizational initiatives reflect organizations' efforts to grapple with a shortage of leadership. In our experience these efforts do not usually arise from a complete understanding of the problem but represent intuitive responses to half-perceived difficulties.

If we assume that leadership is a limited resource, that there are not enough really effective leaders around, then a whole series of organizational initiatives assume a new consistency and rationale. In the short term, the market response for any product or service for which demand is rising faster than supply is that its price rises relative to other prices. Where leaders are seen as a key ingredient in the search for a competitive edge, firms will bid up the price of leaders against each other in order to secure the available supplies. If the supply of leadership is relatively fixed and unresponsive to price the result – for recognized leaders – is huge windfall gains which owe less to leadership performance than their perceived scarcity value.

If many organizations have, in the past, chosen to nurture managers rather than leaders, then the current supply will be limited. In our discussion in Chapter Two the most promising group to provide leaders are the Nomads – the group least likely to have been retained by many large organizations. A shortage of leaders would help to explain the paradox of why executive rewards are rising at a time of unprecedented managerial redundancies.

Such a strategy of buying in leadership is not necessarily successful. Media coverage has revealed repeated instances of highly-rewarded senior executives being ousted when their leadership skills are found to be inadequate. High prices are no guarantee of quality as buyers in all markets eventually discover.

A rising price for leaders is one indicator of shortage but, on its own, it is insufficient. It has been widely suggested that the rise and rise of directors' salaries owes more to the nature and composition of remuneration committees than it does to labour market forces. If there is a real shortage of leaders, if organizations increasingly perceive their performance as being constrained by a lack of leadership, then it is possible, drawing from economics and from constraint theory, to predict organizations' likely responses. These responses do not depend on organizations fully recognizing the nature of the problem. Appropriate responses only require that organizations recognize the symptoms and respond intelligently.

Untapped sources

Conventional economic theory suggests that shortages and higher prices encourage searches for alternative sources of supply. In this instance it predicts that organizations would begin to look beyond their conventional managerial recruiting grounds to prospect for largely untapped sources of supply. Organizations might begin to reassess the leadership potential of women who were overlooked in the search for conventional managers. Organizations may reconsider women who were previously not thought to have managerial potential. Lack of years of experience may not be considered to be such a big disadvantage. Recasting the competences required of leaders may highlight qualities in the operating style of women that are regarded as desirable in modern leaders. Women may be regarded as better interpersonally and better at handling people. These perceptions may not reflect reality. What is interesting is that it is evidence of the search for alternative sources of leadership and recognition of alternative leadership styles. In Chapter Three, we reviewed the evidence of increasing numbers of women managers and directors. Such increases are consistent with a wider search for leadership talent.

A related approach, which we have been involved with for a number of our clients, is to profile the existing managers against the new set of desired leadership competencies. Typically we have done this by seeking feedback from those who work with each individual manager. The feedback is usually gathered via questionnaires which may be specific leadership questionnaires gathering information about the individual's performance in relation to the full range of leadership styles or they might be broader competency-based questionnaires relating to a range of competencies derived for a particular organization of which leadership is just one sub-set. In our experience the more specific questionnaires provide a stronger developmental focus.

Having gathered the information we work at two levels. With each individual manager we help them prepare an individual personal development plan, building on their perceived strengths and development needs. These personal development plans seek to maximize the individual's use of on-the-job development opportunities with suitable coaching and mentoring rather than relying on off-the-job training programmes. With the organization we develop an audit of the organization's current stock of leaders, taking care to protect the confidentiality of each individual respondent. The organizational audit provides a snapshot of the organization's current strengths and development needs in terms of leadership. Working with the organization we construct a systematic development programme to enhance its leadership capacity and thereby remove the constraint.

Developing the existing leadership potential within the organization is a relatively conventional and useful approach. Building that development off the profiling process permits a much more focused process of development for the individuals and the organization. By integrating these two approaches, and accepting that the profiling may identify individuals for whom demanding leadership roles are inappropriate, we offer a more cost-effective targeted approach. The profiling approach also facilitates more feedback later and the creation of a rolling programme of development. Managers are made more aware of the need for continuous improvement rather than one-off 'fixes'.

Exploiting the constraint
The theory of constraints, as expounded by Eli Goldratt in his 1990 work of that title, proposes that, having identified the constraint, the next task is to exploit it. In this context the implications are clear. Those leaders who are available to the organization are given bigger jobs. If there are not enough leaders to go round, those who are available are required to do more and more. The constraining factor is exploited as fully as possible. Delayering the organization demands

much more of the leaders who remain. Widening the spans of control demands more of the leaders and exposes more of the organization to people who actually can lead. Longer working hours, bigger spans of control, more and more change, all testify to organizations' willingness to exploit the leadership constraint. Whether the strategy works depends crucially on the organization's success in putting effective leaders in place. If those holding down the larger jobs are managers, not leaders, the results will be unsatisfactory.

Goldratt further argues that, having identified the constraint and having decided to exploit it, the next stage is to subordinate everything else to that decision. If the constraint is a lack of leadership, then those who are capable of providing leadership should focus on that to the exclusion of all else. Time that leaders spend on non-leadership activities will have a much poorer return than that spent on leadership. If leadership is the key constraint, then only time spent on leadership is worthwhile. Until the leadership constraint is removed, all other considerations are secondary. From our consulting experience, many organizations and the managers/leaders within them have yet to come to terms with the demands of this rule. Many managers are still spending time on other activities rather than using their influence to shift the paradigms of those around them in ways which enable their organization to change successfully. Routine meetings, formal approvals, lengthy reports and responding to organizational demands continue to distract from the leadership role.

Leadership substitutes

A further strategy available to organizations is to find substitutes for leadership so that the demands for leadership can be met in other ways. This requires organizations to devise means of providing leadership without having to rely on higher-paid executives. The last few years have seen a great upsurge of interest in self-directed teams. One reason for that may be that self-directed teams offer a cheaper solution to the leadership constraint. By combining the talents of all the individuals, organizations hope to lessen the demands for leadership from elsewhere. Creating the right climate and culture, providing a vision for the self-directed teams requires high-level leadership skills. Once the fundamental building blocks of organizational culture and team-building are in place, the demands for leadership from outside the team are lessened.

An additional bonus may be that organizations spot previously unrecognized talent operating within the self-directed teams. People who display effective leadership skills inside teams without the benefit of managerial authority or status are worth developing and promoting. They show up a lot earlier than would probably have been the case in a conventional hierarchical organization in which demonstrable leadership was less achievable and less sought after. The trap of promoting people only to discover that they cannot lead is avoided. Only those who can lead are worthy of promotion.

Crisis of leadership

All this builds up a case that suggests that what is actually going on in organizations is an unrecognized crisis of leadership. As the crisis is unrecognized, the response to it lacks consistency and direction. Increasing the reward package, widening spans of control, developing existing managers, introducing self-directed teams – all of these are partial responses to the problem. Failure to investigate differences in values and reward preferences between leaders and managers may result in inappropriately focused reward packages. Widening spans of control may simply impose unacceptable burdens of stress and overwork, unless the organization also provides appropriate development on managing in flattened structures.

Developing existing managers and new recruits needs to be linked to continuing processes of individual improvement. Self-directed teams require considerable support and development and substantial changes in the organization's behaviour if they are to succeed. Each of these initiatives is potentially powerful and helpful. They are much more helpful and powerful if they are all seen as components in an integrated approach to transforming the organization.

The lack of consistency in organizational approaches to leadership is not only reflected in the frequent failure to integrate these various initiatives, the failure to develop coherent approaches to leadership development but also in the handling of redundancies and severances. In managing the processes of redundancy and delayering, many organizations have sought to avoid compulsory dismissals. To achieve the required job cuts organizations have offered various packages of consultancy assignments, pension enhancements and severance packages. Many of these arrangements are aimed primarily at encouraging older, more experienced managers to leave. In some of those organizations it is now rare to encounter managers over the age of fifty. Programmes of this kind have some real advantages in providing individuals with levels of financial security while perhaps creating some opportunities for those stranded further down the career escalator.

Programmes of this kind also have some real disadvantages because of their voluntary nature. Some of those who leave are Rocks whose sense of anger and frustration at the organization makes it impossible for them to continue. Many other Rocks will continue to nestle in their uncomfortable surroundings. Nomads are also likely to quit. Flexible and adventurous, the Nomads regard the financial package as a helpful reduction to the cost of doing what they might have done anyway. From an organizational point of view, faced by a shortage of leadership, this willingness to pay talent to go away makes less sense. If the constraint is that of lack of leadership, subsidizing valuable contributors to quit is recklessly profligate of talent and money.

Fewer promotions

At the same time, two other changes that are taking place inside organizations are making the development of leadership more difficult. One is that the delayering movement restricts conventional opportunities to gain leadership experience. As there are fewer pro-motion positions available, the likelihood of any individual gaining such a promotion and the development opportunity it represents is reduced. In addition, the step from non-leadership to leadership has become much bigger. There are fewer opportunities to lead small teams or groups of staff. Widening spans of control increases the size of the first leadership role. Leading large groups is more demanding than leading small teams. Of course there are opportunities to develop leadership skills within teams in those organizations which have adopted self-directed teams. If organizations have not adopted self-directed teams, then the opportunities for self-development are less.

The rhetoric of empowerment

In addition, many organizations adopted, and transmitted internally, the rhetoric of empowerment. In part that rhetoric encourages values of initiative, self-responsibility, self-direction and self-development. These values are a means of encouraging people to act as their own leaders. One consequence of more self-leadership is fewer demands on the organization and its limited leadership resources. Empowerment has also had an unintended consequence. People's expectations about themselves and their prospects have risen, despite the evidence of delayering and cutbacks. Some of these expectations concern upward career movements.

Many companies are finding themselves caught between two mill-stones. They are busy reducing the number of managerial positions and consequently opportunities for conventional promotions. At the same time, they have unleashed greater demands from those lower down in the organization in terms of expectations about the ability to get promoted, to do new things, to contribute in more significant ways. Many companies are finding themselves on the receiving end of negative reactions from their employees who cannot see the career opportunities they have been encouraged to anticipate. The situation is frequently exacerbated by the performance of old-style command and control managers whose behaviour is evidently at odds with the leadership styles required in an empowering organization.

At one level, these disenchanted employees have reason to feel let down. Traditional career opportunities have been blown away in the gale of structural changes. There are fewer opportunities for advancement. Organizations have a limited number of options in these circumstances. One option might be to suggest that it will all return to normal, that once the recession is over opportunities for promotion will reappear. There is, inevitably, a grain, a very small grain, of truth in that, but employees are unlikely to be sufficiently gullible to forget their concerns. As a second option, organizations might acknowledge the change and its likely permanence but emphasize the rewards for the small minority who do succeed. If enough employees regard being promoted as equivalent to winning the National Lottery they may be willing to offer substantial co-operation and commitment in the belief this will influence the probability of their numbers coming up. Recasting 'Corporate Human Resources' as 'Mystic Meg' may provide much innocent amusement but will not improve overall promotion prospects. A third option would be for companies to acknowledge frankly the changes which have occurred and to engage in an open and constructive debate about the development of alternatives that would maintain organizational competitiveness while enabling employees to exercise real control over their own careers.

Ladders and mountains
A consultancy assignment undertaken by one of the authors of this book explored how staff in a large manufacturing company visualized

career opportunities. Groups were invited to draw pictures of their career options. The results were highly creative and very stark. They drew ladders, for example, where all the bottom rungs had been removed. There was a 20-foot ladder with no rungs on the bottom ten feet. Another group drew a picture of a mountain. On one side of the mountain there were dangerous hairpin bends and red lights, roadworks and stop lights – all kinds of obstacles. On the other side of the mountain, which they saw as graduate recruitment, there was this nice straight road, without any obstacles, that zoomed straight to the top. (The graduates who were present indicated that they saw their situation rather differently.)

The images were then used, together with other material relating to helping and hindering behaviours by managers, the nature of career development etc. at an internal management conference to highlight key issues.

Upward movement

Traditionally, when people talked about managerial careers they were talking about being promoted. Careers were synonymous with upward movements – typically within a function – until a point when the unit being managed was sufficiently large to generate general management status or a position on the board. Successful managers aspired to run operating companies or to achieve corporate-level responsibility.

Some companies insisted on operational experience as well as corporate experience. Large international companies expected at least one overseas posting. Real cross-functional experience was relatively rare. What was really valued was expertise within a particular function or speciality. Genuine functional expertise was commonly the key to promotion – at least according to the formal policies. Consulting experiences indicate that other factors including gender, sports interests, luck, networks and visibility were also believed to play a role.

Functional expertise as a route to promotion increasingly looks like a wasting asset. Organizations are now seeking leadership qualities that are not necessarily strongly related to technical or functional expertise. This throws up some interesting issues for aspiring managers. For one thing, they have to ask themselves whether they have the right skills and behaviours required by today's corporate challenges. Do they have the competencies and the willingness to lead? There is one thing about which they can be sure. It is no longer going to be enough to be technically competent. To win quick promotion managers must seek out opportunities that demonstrate their capacity to influence, to re-frame, to shape people's paradigms and move them forward.

However, that is not the complete picture. Because of the increasing pressure of global competition and the need for companies to be really competitive, technical competence is going to remain a key issue. Companies are always going to need people who keep up-to-date technically. Increasingly, such people are unlikely to be promoted to the higher reaches of the organization unless they have the leadership skills as well. Being highly competent should remain a necessary condition for advancement but, without effective leadership skills, it will be insufficient. The challenge then for organizations and individuals is how to develop, hone and improve their leadership without the incentive of likely promotion.

For some managers this may not be a problem. They may simply enjoy being experts. They may in the past have only sought promotion because that was what everyone expected of them and it was the only way to get more money and status. The probability of such one-dimensional experts reaching the top of the hierarchy is now remote even though the rewards for getting there are much greater.

The challenge is how to stay up-to-date. This is where the issue of self-development and organizational development becomes a key concern. Individuals who are really keen to stay in the forefront of their areas of expertise will need to be looking constantly for leading-edge companies that will take them on board. Obvious examples are those electronics companies developing state-of-the-art products. They may not pay very well, but they provide opportunities to work with really talented people. They, in turn, provide learning experiences that can further careers.

Learning from others
Effective leadership in times of change requires the ability to learn quickly and the skills to enable others to learn quickly as well. Quite a lot is known about the way people learn. We know, for example, that the times managers learn most is when they take on new jobs and tasks they are not really sure how to do. They go through an enormous upheaval. They experience the full gamut of emotions, from being absolutely panic-stricken to being lost in

the fog until they begin to get some kind of handle on the new responsibility. At that stage they start to make progress and things begin to fall into place. Novel, challenging assignments are very powerful development experiences.

The kind of people one works with can also be an important influence on learning experiences. What are these people like? How good are they technically in terms of what they do? Are they really competent? Are they really expert? Do they really have something to offer?

Equally important is how they work together. If they are all expert and keep their expertise to themselves it will be very difficult to learn from them. Leaders and their associates – peers, direct reports, clients, superiors – need to share some generosity of spirit if they are to learn from each other. Leaders who are generous with what they already know – and do not know – make it easier for other people to develop. When considering developmental assignments there are vital questions to ask about the other people involved. Are they generous of spirit? Do they actually want to push out the boundaries? Are they prepared to listen to ideas and challenge and confront? Are they too busy hoarding their existing knowledge? Are they too frightened to confront the challenges?

When looking for another career-enhancing role – be it a new job, a role in a project team, or a difficult assignment – there are many dimensions to consider. Some of these concern the competence of the others, some the nature of the working climate and some their generosity. Another consideration concerns access to the outside world through clients, customers, suppliers, competitors. In a highly competitive world relying on internal stimuli for learning is limiting and dangerous. Clients who are at the leading edge in their own markets, competitors who are rated best-in-class, suppliers who work with really tough competitors, provide great learning opportunities for those with the courage and ability to seize them.

What all this amounts to is the fact that there is much greater diversity than there used to be when considering the career path to pursue. In the past moving one's own expertise forward while climbing the managerial hierarchy was possible and desirable. At some stage managerial responsibilities might conflict with technical or functional expertise. At that point managers confronted stark choices about what really mattered to them. For many expertise was preferable to greater managerial responsibility.

In today's climate, those kinds of choices are likely to come earlier and are likely to be much starker. Running any large team will make constant and continuing demands on your leadership. Technical expertise may be of more significance to other team members. A key aspect of the leadership role is the need to generate a climate and culture that supports learning by all members of the team.

Capacity for leadership

The Manufacturing Vision Group, a collection of leading academic and business people who studied product development projects in a number of major companies in the US, concluded that the best way to develop managers was to put them in charge of specific internal projects. The group declared in the *Harvard Business Review*:

'The challenge for companies is both to find and develop the right kind of people and to expand significantly their capacity for leadership. The challenge is to understand what leadership requires of people and to create a process and a system in which leaders develop naturally as part of the life of the business.

'Not everyone will be a leader, but leaders will emerge naturally as part of the normal growth and development within the company. Leading projects will become the way one develops as a general manager. Over time, the ranks of the senior executives will be filled by people with a rich background of getting things done through projects.'

This view is borne out by research by the Institute of Management (IM), outlined in its publication, *Management Development to the Millennium – The New Priorities*. It says that by 2001 the manager will no longer be The Boss, but a team leader who will earn the respect of all his people. It also maintains that in the changing employment market individual managers are increasingly likely to be employed on a contract, interim or temporary basis. The twenty-first-century manager will need to be adaptable and have up-to-date knowledge, together with flexible and transferable skills. Those who wish to keep their jobs must think strategically and be prepared to train and re-train throughout their working lives. Portfolio careers, comprising a variety of different jobs demanding varied skills, are likely to be the way forward.

The Institute of Employment Studies (IES) says devolved and delayered organizations and the subsequent reduction in opportunites for promotion are demanding new approaches to defining and delivering development. One of the most popular current initiatives, according to the IM, is the 'personal development plan', but issues have been raised about whether organizations are genuinely willing to consider the 'whole person' or just the 'employee in their current job'. The IES says:

'We help companies examine their whole approach to careers by facilitating events with senior line managers at which they examine the links between business priorities and problems and their career development. Having produced an agenda for areas for change, they then go on and re-engineer various career processes – succession planning, individual career planning, development programmes and the link with succession.'

The key issue facing aspiring managers today is not just that there are fewer opportunities and consequently more competition. It is not just that career ladders have become shorter and more slippery. The real issue is that the requirements for effective management have altered. Organizations now need far more leaders in their available managerial posts. This need for leadership changes the promotion criteria, the desired competencies and the relevant experiences. The new leadership skills appear to be in short supply – judging by the number of *ad hoc* and expensive measures organizations have undertaken. Lots of people who thought they were going to have managerial careers because they have degrees or technical expertise are going to be disappointed. The indication is that unless prospective managers have a full complement of leadership skills and a real commitment to continuing development – for themselves and others – their prospects of promotion are very slim indeed.

Chapter Five
Designing Careers for Employability

Aspiring managers need a new way of defining and designing their own careers, which basically requires them to be clear about their own potential and the extent to which they believe in that potential, about how they develop that potential and how much further they can progress. They also need to be clear about how much effort they are prepared to put in, in relation to the corporate systems in which they are working; they should understand their own career anchors, what it is they really seek from work and the values and the context in which they are likely to be most comfortable and most productive. They must be aware of all these factors. They need clarity about their own expectations of themselves and about others' expectations of them and the extent to which those expectations sustain or diminish further development. They must also realize that their real concern should be about learning and development to maximize their employability. They should be aiming for employability, rather than upward progression.

One manager could stay in the same company for forty years and perform such a wide range of jobs, assignments and projects that she was always employable. Not only would she always be employable by her own company, she would always have been attractive to other employers because of her immediate, marketable skills. Another manager might have moved from company to company and spent forty years always doing the same job. He timed his entries and exits in a way in which they were always just right for the company he joined and his skills were appropriate and needed while he was with them, but he effectively did the same job all the time. One might look at a particular manager's career record and be amazed by all the companies he or she has worked with, whilst another manager may only have worked for the same company all his or her life. The latter career path may seem utterly uninspired but in reality that manager may have done thirty different jobs in a 40-year career with one company; while the other manager has really done the same job in thirty different companies.

Managers ambitious for continuing employability need to explore the conditions in which they are most likely to learn and develop. What are the circumstances which allow them to do that and how would they recognize them? They need to consider the tools they will require. How might they understand their own potential? How might they recognize their current state of development? How might they evaluate their own willingness to make the effort to develop and the extent to which external factors influence that willingness? How do they reach a real awareness of what it is they want from work in terms of personal fulfilment, of what values they are expressing in their work? How do they recognize those circumstances in which their own values and those of potential employing organizations are aligned or misaligned? What do they understand about their own learning patterns? What really does contribute to increasing their employability? Learning has to be marketable in the sense that it has to be related to opportunities in the outside world. Otherwise, learning – however valuable aesthetically – will yield nothing in employability terms because the managers have not identified a market for their learning.

Career resilience

Robert H. Waterman Jr, Judith A. Waterman and Betsy A. Collard, the authors of a *Harvard Business Review* article about the need for organizations to develop a career-resilient workforce, describe self-assessment as 'a systematic process of taking stock of those attitudes that influence one's effectiveness, success, and happiness'.★

They go on to say 'Unless individuals understand the environments

★ Excerpts from 'Toward a Career-Resilient Workforce', by Robert H. Waterman Jr, Judith A. Waterman and Betsy A. Collard, published in the July-August 1994 issue, are reprinted in Chapters Five, Six and Eight by permission of *Harvard Business Review*. Copyright © 1994 by the President and Fellows of Harvard College; all rights reserved.

that let them shine, the interests that ignite them and the skills that help them excel, how can they choose a company or job where they can make their greatest contribution? Unless they understand how their personal style affects others, how can they function with maximum effectiveness? Knowing yourself is the first step towards becoming career resilient.'

John O'Brien, who runs his own London-based career advisory consultancy, has some unorthodox techniques for persuading managers to undergo in-depth personal assessments. He asks them to imagine in their mind's eye that they are going into a church. The church is full of people and it is apparent that a funeral is in progress: 'You walk up to the coffin and lift the lid and discover yourself inside. Then one of the people from the congregation stands up during the service and starts to talk about you, your family and how you lived your life. What would you want them to say about you?'

Often, O'Brien finds, this exercise can have a dramatic impact. It helps people to focus on their true values, divorced from the emotions of the moment. He says: 'Emotions are terribly important, but it helps people get their ducks in a row in terms of what really matters to them. I gave this exercise to one guy who was supposed to be coming for a whole series of counselling sessions with me. He said it was absolutely brilliant. It had changed his life and he didn't need any more counselling, thank you!'

One of the authors of this book has counselled managers from a wide range of industries, using a mixture of psychometric instruments, feedback from colleagues and discussion about their current and future roles. Some managers – a minority – are very self-aware and purposeful in their actions. For them counselling frequently focused on those aspects of their own behaviour that were causing them difficulty or inhibiting them from achieving their full potential. For many others, developing their own self-awareness was a vital first step. Working with a very successful corporate lawyer with a large multinational, the real issue was the conflict he was not handling between his desire to exercise his professional skills and the demands of managing his own staff. Helping him to confront that conflict was the key to enabling him to move forward.

From that work we derived the 'Star of Successfully Self-Managed Careers' which reflected the interplay of five different factors:

THE STAR OF SUCCESSFULLY SELF-MANAGED CAREERS

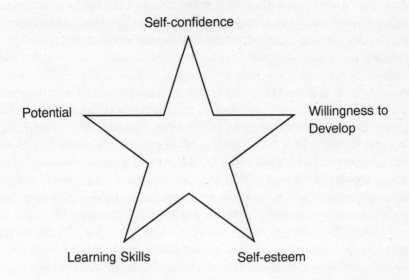

Self-confidence

Potential

Willingness to Develop

Learning Skills

Self-esteem

Learning Skills encompasses the familiar material on learning styles and learning cycles but goes beyond that to probe individuals' readiness to learn. In our experience readiness to learn is the crucial factor. Managers who are content with their current level of performance have little incentive or apparent facility to learn. Those who are aware of shortcomings in their current performance but are unable to bring themselves to acknowledge those gaps frequently resolve that personal dilemma by blaming others for any performance problems. Occasionally one meets managers who appear to believe that, in acknowledging some scope for learning and development, they are labelling themselves as incompetent. Reluctant to accept such labelling, these managers disqualify themselves from developing. Those who are able to acknowledge shortcomings in their current performance, or can perceive future gaps more readily, find and seize learning opportunities.

Self-confidence relates to the individual's belief in their own ability and potential. Managers with a strong sense of self-confidence are much more willing to take on challenging assignments and difficult situations because of their belief in their ability to cope. For some individuals a growing self-confidence arising from their positive experience of managing people is crucial to their development as managers. Self-confidence, in our experience, is a crucial ingredient in managers' development because of its role in enabling them to seize opportunities. Well-founded self-confidence enables a manager to utilize his full range of talents in response to changing circumstances. Of course, a sense of self-confidence that exaggerates the underlying abilities is likely, at some stage, to have a bruising confrontation with reality.

Self-esteem is concerned with the extent to which an individual values whatever it is that he does. A manager who finds herself dealing more and more with people issues that she feels are unimportant compared with the more technical aspects of her work is likely to experience falling self-esteem. Being good at an activity is no guarantee that performing that activity results in positive self-esteem. For some who are promoted to managerial positions being seen to be good at managing may be inadequate compensation for the constraints that the positions impose. The issue for the individual manager is to reach a clearer understanding of her own values in order to recognize those situations that will yield positive self-esteem. It seems most likely that managers will be most inclined to develop those competences that generate positive self-esteem.

Willingness to Develop describes the individual's inclination to make the necessary sacrifices to develop herself. All development is a form of investment. All investment requires the sacrifice of current consumption. The sacrifices managers make may include their personal private time through additional study or through taking on new responsibilities. It may involve a loss of their personal comfort zones by demanding they work in areas with which they are less familiar and in which, consequently, they feel more exposed. It may involve accepting a lower salary in order to obtain desired experience. Some individuals are much more willing to make these sacrifices than others. In part the willingness to make such sacrifices depends on the expected paybacks. Older managers, who have less time to recoup their investments, may be less willing to develop themselves because they see the paybacks as being inadequate. From an economic perspective, these calculations can be projected in terms of costs, expected income streams and discount rates. In reality, given the uncertainties of future income streams because of employment insecurity, differences in individuals' willingness to develop may reflect more on basic psychological differences than on carefully graduated differences in prospective returns. In terms of the Desert

Scene of Chapter Two, Nomads seem much more willing to develop themselves than Rocks. Nomads, one suspects, are less influenced by the current costs of investment in terms of the sacrifices and more attracted to the possible future returns – psychological as well as financial – of wider experience.

Potential is used here to define the individual's latent talent; it is an insight into what the individual could achieve. Self-confidence reflects the individual's belief in her own ability or potential. Potential here is a more objective measure. Individuals may be self-confident without any clear understanding of the particular range and set of talents that they possess. Other individuals may have a good awareness of their own talents but lack the self-belief to exploit them to the full.

Real insight

The appeal of assessment or development centres for many managers is that they provide, for the first time in many cases, real data, insight, and feedback to contribute to the manager's understanding of his own strengths and weaknesses. Such centres are very focused on managers' potential in relation to managerial careers. Of course the data, the insight and the feedback are only as good as the techniques and people employed in the assessment process. For most managers this process is a great deal better than their own attempts to decode the obscure images portrayed by their own reflections on what they have done and what they might have done.

Galaxy of expectations

The Star of Successfully Self-managed Careers does not sit alone in the firmament. It rests in a galaxy of expectations. Some of those expectations are self-generated by the manager. The great majority are externally provided. There is significant evidence from many different fields that high expectations, internal and external, generate high performances. The issue for the manager wishing to maximize employability is to seek out those organizations that have high positive expectations of their staff and who demand that their expectations are met. They do not regard self-development as a 'nice to have'; they demand that their staff develop and go on developing.

Personal development plan

In conventional wisdom, the outcome of all this self-evaluation is that you go away and write your personal development plan and set about attacking the weaknesses. More importantly, it helps you to come to terms with your strengths. People aren't necessarily very good judges of their own ability. They may carry baggage from childhood about what they are good or bad at which is totally mistaken.

Organizations can be crucial in terms of supporting or obstructing the processes that enable individuals to understand themselves more clearly and crucial in shaping the expectations that individuals have about themselves. Many organizations rely very heavily on the performance review process to enable individuals to develop clearer impressions of their strengths, their development needs and of the expectations that the organization has of them. Discussions with many managers and with human resource professionals suggest that, in many cases, performance review processes are, in practice, inadequate for the demands being made upon them. The inadequacy arises from two sources.

Firstly, many managers are reluctant to confront fully areas of poor performance. For a variety of reasons managers, even when reviewing other managers, fail to convey accurately and comprehensively their concerns about performance and/or behaviour. Secondly, even good committed line managers have difficulty judging potential. In part this arises from the very real difficulty of assessing potential which is likely to be seen differently by different people. It also arises from the constraints within which the appraised currently performs. To use a sports team analogy, the manager doing the performance review usually has only seen the appraised playing in one position. To judge potential, the manager also needs the imagination to consider how else the individual might perform in different circumstances. Some sports players have failed to realize their potential until coached by someone perceptive enough to see that they are playing in the 'wrong' position or competing in the 'wrong' event. Individuals look forward to development centres to make up the deficiencies of the performance review system.

Personal values and drivers
There is a lot more to career progression than simply training and development. When talking to individuals about their understanding of career paths, some of their concerns revolve around the nature of employment stability, about whether or not they stay in a company or whether they stay in a particular profession or job. Other concerns relate to what they are doing with their life and whether or not this is

really what they want to do. Edgar Schein, a professor of management at the Massachusetts Institute of Technology in the US, has coined the term 'career anchors' to describe the fact that different people have different key values. Schein points out that what people are trying to do with their life and work is to find a way to live the values that are important to them. For some individuals this may involve having a number of different jobs. For others it may involve staying very much within one occupation, within one profession. Career anchors provide a different insight into career management.

The traditional paradigm around career management is that individuals develop career objectives – usually involving upward movement in the hierarchy – that they pursue subject to a number of constraints, some internal and some external. The perspective that career anchors offer is that people are trying to play out their own strong personal values and drivers. They are only really fulfilled when they find ways to achieve that. The values that people seek to live out are not normally articulated. Indeed, our experience in counselling suggests that many individuals are only partially aware of their values. But it is the effort to live out values, not the pursuit of objectives, that really shapes careers.

Schein has found eight key career anchors (see page 71). One of these, technical or functional competence, describes someone who likes being an expert, who likes being good at something and welcomes the opportunity to exercise his particular expertise. Such people are delighted to be offered a problem that challenges their expertise, because they then have to perform at a higher level in order to come up with an answer. In the past, such people could be described as the bread and butter of large organizations, combined with those, Schein argues, who are really interested in security and stability.

Entrepreneurial types

Today, large organizations are seeking people with different sorts of values. They seek people who are more risk-taking and are more willing to take initiatives. Their search for such people may be frustrated because, Schein argues, those who are really entrepreneurial want to run their own businesses. They may work for organizations for a short period while they learn, but they really want to go it alone. It seems clear that organizations are going to have to provide entrepreneurial types with more opportunities to live their values if they are to retain them. In an attempt to tackle this issue, some companies have introduced the idea of *intra*preneurism, referring to people with entrepreneurial flair but who are still prepared to work within a corporation. In addition, many organizations are beginning to see more benefit in breaking themselves into many smaller units, each of which can be run as a separate small business.

Such opportunities cannot be provided within the old hierarchical structures. Entrepreneurial types cannot be retained within the old patterns of career development with their 'experience blocks' and their queuing systems. Part of the problem is that the old structures of career development assume that what people want out of careers is basically the same. If all managers had broadly similar needs then one structure and one system would be sufficient. Such an assumption of uniformity appears to be without any real foundation.

The challenge facing organizations is how to develop sufficient career opportunities to meet the needs of all the different people it engages and fulfil the organization's own objectives.

Career anchors
The concept of career anchors originally arose from a study designed to understand better how managerial careers evolved and how people learned the values and procedures of their employing organizations. A longitudinal study of forty-four alumni of the master's programme at the Sloan School of Management in the US was initiated in 1961. The original interviews and surveys of values and attitudes were conducted in 1961, 1962 and 1963 while the respondents were second-year students in the two-year master's programme. Then, all were interviewed at their places of work six months after graduation and again one year after graduation. These interviews revealed a great deal about the problems of making the transition from school to work organizations.

All respondents completed questionnaires five years after gradua-tion and had follow-up interviews in 1973, after they were approxi-mately ten to twelve years into their careers. From these sources came insights into how the internal career evolves. The 1973 interviews elicited a detailed chronological career history, asking respondents not only to identify key choices and events, but also to speculate about why they had made those particular choices and how they felt about each change. The interview format was developed by Schein to arrive at the career anchors that are now used to help managers all over the world focus on the important features of their careers.

The actual events of the career histories proved to be highly varied, but the reasons respondents gave for their choices and the pattern of their feelings about events proved to be surprisingly consistent. For each individual, underlying themes, of which he or she had often been unaware, reflected a growing sense of self, based on the learnings of the early years. When these people tried jobs that did not feel right for them, they referred to the image of being pulled back to something that fitted better – hence the metaphor of an anchor.

Based on this longitudinal study and on subsequent career history interviews of several hundred people in various career stages, Edgar Schein identified the eight career anchor categories:

- Technical/functional competence
- General managerial competence
- Autonomy/independence
- Security/stability
- Entrepreneurial creativity
- Sense of service, dedication to a cause
- Pure challenge
- Lifestyle

Schein, who has set out his findings in a useful booklet, *Career Anchors – discovering your real values*, published by Drake Beam Morin, the worldwide outplacement and career management group, maintains that everyone is concerned to some degree with each of these issues. The label 'career anchor' indicates an area of such paramount importance to a person that he or she would not give it up. The person comes to define his or her basic self-image in terms of that concern and it becomes an overriding issue at every stage of the career. Schein defines the eight career anchors as follows:

Technical/functional competence
Some people discover as their careers unfold that they have both a strong talent and high motivation for a particular kind of work. What really turns them on is the exercise of their talent and the satisfaction of knowing that they are experts. This can happen in

71

any kind of work. For example, an engineer may discover that he or she is very good at design; a sales person may find real selling talent; a manufacturing manager may encounter greater and greater pleasure in running complex plants; a financial analyst may uncover talent and enjoyment in solving complex capital investment problems; a teacher may enjoy his or her growing expertise in the field.

As these people move along in their careers they notice that if they are moved into other areas of work they are less satisfied and less skilled. They begin to feel pulled back to their areas of competence and enjoyment. They build a sense of identity around the *content* of their work – the technical or functional areas in which they are succeeding – and develop increasing skills in those areas.

General managerial competence

Some people – but only some – discover as their careers progress that they really want to become general managers, that management *per se* interests them, that they have the range of competence that is required to be a general manager, and that they have the ambition to rise to organizational levels where they will be responsible for major policy decisions and where their own efforts will make the difference between success and failure.

Members of this group differ from the technical/functional people in that they view specialization as a trap. They recognize the necessity to know several functional areas well and they accept that one must be expert in one's business or industry to function well in a general manager's job. Key values and motives for this group of people are advancement up the corporate ladder to higher levels of responsibility, opportunities for leadership, contributions to the success of their organizations and high income.

Autonomy/independence

Some people discover early in their working lives that they cannot stand to be bound by other people's rules, procedures, working hours, dress codes and other norms that almost invariably arise in any kind of organization. Regardless of what they work on, such people have an overriding need to do things in their own way, at their own pace, and to their own standards. They find organizational life to be restrictive, irrational and intrusive into their private lives; therefore, they prefer to pursue more independent careers on their own terms. If forced to make a choice between a present job that

72

permits autonomy and a higher grade job that requires giving it up, the autonomy/independence-anchored person would stay in his or her present job.

Security/stability

Some people have an overriding need to organize their careers so that they feel safe and secure, so that future events are predictable, and so that they can relax in the knowledge that they have made it. Everyone needs some degree of security and stability throughout life; at certain life stages financial security can become the overriding issue, such as when one is raising and educating a family or approaching retirement. However, for some people security and stability are predominant throughout their careers to the point that these concerns guide and constrain all major career decisions.

Such people often seek jobs in organizations that provide job tenure, that have the reputation of avoiding layoffs, that have good retirement plans and benefit programmes, and that have the image of being strong and reliable. For this reason, government and civil service jobs are often attractive to these people. They obtain some of their self-satisfaction from identifying with their organizations even if they do not have high-ranking or important jobs.

Entrepreneurial creativity

Some people discover early in life that they have an overriding need to create new businesses of their own by developing new products or services, by building new organizations through financial manipulation or by taking over existing businesses and reshaping them to their own specifications. These are not necessarily only inventors or creative artists, although some of them at times become entrepreneurs. Nor should these people be confused with creative researchers, market analysts or advertising executives. The creative urge in this group is specifically towards creating new organizations, products or services that can be identified with the entrepreneur's own efforts, that will survive on their own and that will be economically successful. Making money is then a measure of success.

Sense of service, dedication to a cause

Some people enter occupations because of central values that they want to embody in their work. They are oriented more towards

73

these values than towards the actual talents or areas of competence involved. Their career decisions are based on the desire to improve the world in some fashion. Those in the helping professions – such as medicine, nursing, social work, teaching and the ministry – are typically considered to hold this career anchor. However, dedication to a cause clearly also characterizes some people in business management and in organizational careers. Some examples include the human resource specialist who works on affirmative action programmes, the labour lawyer intent on improving labour-management relations, the research scientist working on a new drug, or the manager who chooses to go into public service in order to improve some aspect of society in general. Values such as working with people, serving humanity and helping one's nation can be powerful anchors in one's career.

However, not everyone in a service-oriented occupation is motivated by the desire to serve. Some doctors, lawyers, ministers and social workers may be anchored in technical/functional competence or autonomy or security; some may want to become general managers. Without knowing which anchor is actually operating, one will not know what the career occupant really wants.

Pure challenge
Some people anchor their careers in the perception that they can conquer anything or anybody. They define success as overcoming impossible obstacles, solving unsolvable problems or winning out over extremely tough opponents. As they progress, they seek ever tougher challenges. For some this takes the form of seeking jobs in which they face more and more difficult problems. However, these people are not technically/functionally anchored because they seem not to care in what area the problem occurs. Some high-level strategy/management consultants seem to fit this pattern in that they relish more and more difficult kinds of strategic assignments.

For others, the challenge is defined in interpersonal and competitive terms. For example, some naval aviators perceive their sole purpose in life to be to prepare themselves for the ultimate confrontation with an enemy. In that confrontation these 'warriors' would prove to themselves and to the world their superiority in competitive combat. Although the military version of this anchor may seem somewhat over-dramatised, other people also define life in competitive terms. Many sales people, professional athletes, and even some managers define their careers essentially as daily combat or competition in which winning is everything.

Lifestyle
At first glance this concept seems like a contradiction in terms. People who organize their existence around lifestyle are, in one sense, saying that their careers are less important to them and therefore that they do not have a career anchor. They belong in a discussion of career anchors, however, because a growing number of people who are highly motivated towards meaningful careers are, at the same time, adding the condition that the career must be integrated with total lifestyle. This is not merely a matter of balancing personal and professional lives as many people have traditionally done; it is more a matter of finding a way to integrate the needs of the individual, the family and the career.

Because such an integration is itself an evolving function, this kind of person wants flexibility more than anything else. Unlike the autonomy-anchored person who also wants flexibility, those with lifestyle anchors are quite willing to work for organizations provided that the right options are available at the right time. Such options might include travelling or moving only at times when family situations permit, part-time work if life concerns require it, sabbaticals, paternity and maternity leaves, day-care options (which are becoming especially relevant for the growing population of dual-career couples and single parents), flexible working hours, working at home during normal working hours and so on. Lifestyle-anchored people look more for an organizational attitude than a specific programme – an attitude that reflects respect for personal and family concerns and that makes genuine re-negotiation of the psychological contract possible.

Hooked on a career
John O'Brien, the independent career counsellor, has had a lot of experience of helping managers unravel their career aspirations: 'All sorts of things come out of the discussions about people's insecurities, aspirations, needs, pressures and so on. There are so many dimensions in terms of somebody's in a job and they're hooked on it. I recently had a guy for an assessment for a senior appointment in tears. He started off fairly cool about it, saying he had been headhunted for the job and that he wouldn't have gone forward if there wasn't more

than a 50–50 chance of getting it. By the end of it the guy had been tearful on five occasions and it was quite clear he was totally miserable where he was but stuck into the economic slavery of a big package, mortgage, wife, children, all the commitments – and he couldn't get out of them. I see a lot of frustration, unhappiness, but no opportunity for people to take stock and talk privately about it and make decisions for themselves. You can't do it in-house.

'People get lost. Everyone has his or her own reasons, but there is a common pattern: "I've done this sort of work for a number of years and I've moved around within the company, but I really don't want to go on doing this. I've had enough of it. I'm typecast now. How can I break out of it? What is it that's really important?"'

Such desperate thoughts can easily lead to bad career decisions unless there is somebody on hand like O'Brien to steer the unfortunate manager in the right direction: 'I remember counselling a guy who was with a big financial institution – he's now got a super job abroad actually. But he was at the point of saying he wanted to be a consultant and do his own thing.'

O'Brien conducted a standard personality test on the man and reached the conclusion that this was the last career move this person should take given his personality type. He took O'Brien's advice and was eternally grateful to him: 'We talked for two hours and he said it was the most sensible conversation he had ever had. Somehow the process of just talking out loud, working out what's important, where you want to go, what are your strengths and weaknesses, what do you like and what don't you like, what do you want to get out of life, helps people to focus on where they're going.

'There are two aspects to it. There's the element of what it is that suits you and your personality and what you really want to get out of life. Then there is the practical stock-taking. It sometimes pays, for example, to do a real health check in terms of people's finances and challenge them from a financial point of view, so they realize the risks they're taking. Once you've done that, people just have to take the plunge.'

Susan Bloch, a psychologist and senior consultant with London-based career counsellors GHN, helps top executives to manage their careers and themselves more effectively: 'We work on issues such as managing relationships, communicating, networking, assertiveness and time management. Alongside this, people look at their careers, understand what their skills and strengths are, what needs further developing, and build up the strength to move to the next stage. Typically, people bulldoze into new roles, brag about what they did at the last company and don't think about establishing communications with the key people who will help them make a success.'

Carol Pemberton, a consultant at Sundridge Park Management Centre, argues that the real measure of success should be job satisfaction: 'We are moving away from the idea of a successful career being something you can measure by job title and salary to people being involved in things that have meaning for them.' She advocates the development of the 'internal CV': 'People have to become much better at monitoring themselves and assessing their needs; asking if they're doing something they value, if their being there has made a difference, how much they have learned. They need to see themselves as their own best resource, and build "career resilience". Find out where opportunities are growing and declining in your organization, what the priorities are for senior management. That will tell you whether the area you are in is vulnerable or if there are key projects coming that will give you visibility and opportunities for development.'

Job shift
David Clutterbuck, the leading management author and expert on mentoring, has identified a new technique called 'job shift' as the means to advance in the flattened pyramid. In the former hierarchical organization, he points out, jobs were very prescribed within clearly defined boundaries within specified grades. Promotion occurred when someone at a senior level considered that the job incumbent had gained the experience that fitted him or her for the next vertical grade. This conventional approach no longer works in today's delayered organizations. Ambitious managers have to be far more subtle.

The job shift theory suggests that the way to do it is gradually to enlarge the scope of your present job until you stretch the boundaries and eventually break into new territories of work by getting to understand the thinking and operating methods of the person or people at the next level up. You continue to perform the core duties of your existing job and continue to be paid for working at that level, but the content of the job slowly shifts. The shape of the job changes as you take over an increasing number of responsibilities outside the boundaries of your existing work.

Eventually your job becomes diamond-shaped as you are half in your original job and half into the next level up. The breakthrough comes when somebody at a senior level recognizes that you have acquired the skills and the knowledge to move up a grade. You have engineered your own promotion.

This process is further precipitated by steadily delegating the work you inherit to lower levels of the organization. Clutterbuck reckons that a smart manager can delegate, make obsolete or generally dispose of, at least 25 per cent of the inherited job in the first year of taking over, simply by changing things around and bringing in new systems and people. In the second year the manager should be able to get rid of a further 25 per cent of the job because by then he or she will have trained staff to take on the less demanding aspects of the job. He adds:

'In year three, by the combination of quality systems and people involvement, you actually get people working on the tasks themselves using their creativity, so you should be able to get rid of another 25 per cent of the job. So in managing this transition, what you're actually trying to do is give yourself space to work at the next level, either in terms of breadth if that's appropriate or in terms of depth. What most people do, of course, is hang on to everything in their job, but the guys who are smart try and delegate. You either systematize it or you delegate as much of your job as you can. So in three years you should only have about 25 per cent of your original job left, which puts you in a position to move on.'

There is an art to manipulating the job shift approach to your advantage. 'One of the keys is how well you understand the thinking of the next level up. If you don't understand what drives the people at the next level to make the decisions they do, you can't actually get on their wavelength. Secondly, you need to move the boundaries of your job, change its shape, at every possible opportunity, so that if anything new comes along in terms of a project, even if it is only a small project, you should grab it if you think it is going to add to your net value within the organization. It is much more valuable to have a mixture of things you have worked on or taken responsibility for, plus some specialization. You need to decide what knowledge and capabilities would be really useful for you in terms of career development.

'It might, for example, be very helpful to have a foreign language capability, so you would have an education goal and a reading goal to learn about the areas you want to get into. Quite a few people are picking up on the Internet, for example. You become the company's expert on the Internet. That brings you to notice and helps further your career. Suddenly you become manager of a department to pursue that goal for the whole company. It's a question of seizing those kinds of opportunities, looking for areas in which you can become an expert.

'The useful thing about becoming an expert in a particular area is that when you decide it is not going to take you any further you can move on to being an expert in something else. But you can still keep your former expertise ticking over by reading the occasional article, for example, and you can bring it out of the cupboard whenever the subject comes up.'

Mentoring

Mentoring, in David Clutterbuck's view, can provide an extra boost to the job shift strategy, because it can be an aid to transition: 'We are defining mentoring now as helping people through transitions in work, career or life. The mentor can champion your cause and help you to locate and select the kind of projects that will help the job shift process.

'What's quite interesting about mentoring at the moment is that we have found an enormous gulf growing between American and British mentoring. American mentoring is about sponsorship and the mentor is very powerful. You are the young person who is supposed to sit at the guru's feet. It's all about career development, whereas in the UK, mentoring is more about personal development and the development of the individual.'

The American style is directive. The UK style tends to have a counselling approach, which is in line with the idea that managers today need to be more proactive in developing their own careers, while needing a lot of support from the organization in terms of the learning tools they require to become more self-reliant. Facilitating, networking and empowerment all play a part to varying degrees in this more self-determining approach to career management. Says Clutterbuck: 'People who are managing their careers properly are deciding the sort of help they need and who in the organization can provide that help – not necessarily because they are the most powerful, but because they can learn from them. In some of the most effective mentoring relationships that we've seen, the mentor has been less senior in the organization than the mentee.'

The directive style of mentoring can work to the detriment of the organization. Powerful figures who bestow their patronage on a protégé (a term which runs counter to the age of empowerment) often choose people who are like themselves. For example, aggressive, competitive, task-focused managers are going to choose someone who reminds them of themselves twenty years ago. The trend, however, is starting to go in the opposite direction. The mentees themselves are doing the choosing. They look out for someone who is going to support their personal career goals. As Clutterbuck says:

'It is becoming much more legitimate to approach someone and to ask him or her to become your mentor. The key factor that makes the difference between whether you get accepted or not is being very clear about why you want it, what you are trying to achieve.'

Some organizations are using mentors to gather information about aspiring managers and feed it back to them. This used to be done largely through performance appraisal, but as organizations become more project-based there is no regular line manager to gather the relevant information. Managers often spend only a few months under a project leader before moving on to the next task force. Mentors can act as a central point to accumulate the data from different parts of the organization:

'The mentor doesn't make any judgements,' says Clutterbuck, 'but puts the data together and presents it back to you and helps talk you through it and look at the developmental issues behind that. I think it's a very good scheme.'

Managing Employability

One of the techniques we use to help managers appreciate their own situations and the extent to which they have imposed their own constraints on their options is the 'Golden Rules' exercise. This involves asking managers to advise a well-liked, respected friend who has just joined their organization on the informal rules for getting promoted. The most common responses revolve around the need to fit in, gain visibility with those who are influential and support the hierarchy. Managers are, simultaneously, aware that such rules are inappropriate if their organizations are to survive. As individuals, however, many continue to act as if they believe that their future prospects depend more on their observing the informal golden rules than by developing their employability.

Managing one's career through employability rather than advancement is understood at an intellectual level by most managers as an appropriate response to the loss of employment security. At an emotional level many managers continue to feel that organizations should provide careers and that if they are loyal they will be rewarded. This is not entirely surprising. Many managers were recruited some time ago. Despite the recent job cuts and delayering, it is still common to work with groups of managers where most have been with their current employer for at least a decade. They are the survivors. Many would feel that they survived because they managed the organization rather than their employability. Managing employability involves managers in continual risk-taking. Clutterbuck's notion of 'Job Shift' would have major appeal to a Nomad. Many Rocks would see it as close to organizational insurrection. For them jobs change when the organization decrees that jobs change, not as a result of individual initiative and decision-making and development of others.

Maximizing employability requires managers to stretch themselves continuously. Effective self-career management involves the simultaneous extension of one's self-confidence, self-esteem, learning skills, willingness to develop and potential. Little wonder that many managers would prefer to leave it to their organizations.

Chapter Six
Creating an Open Market

A survey of twelve leading UK organizations undergoing major change programmes was conducted between October 1994 and April 1995 by Future Perfect, the consultancy and counselling group for organizations and people in transition. The organizations scrutinized ranged from Shell, Royal Mail and IBM to Marks & Spencer, the RAC and HM Prison Service. The survey focused particularly on the impact of delayering and noted that a typical view of organizations is that a deterioration in staff morale is a necessary sacrifice to maintain competitiveness. The possible impact on the organization's *future* competitiveness tends not to be a preoccupation, suggests the report. However, much current literature suggests that the price may be substantial, particularly in two areas:

- *Innovation*: the untrusting reaction of staff who have experienced downsizing may in fact inhibit the growth of the innovative and responsive culture which is likely to be required for future competitiveness.
- *Customer Relations*: undergoing that experience may have a permanent impact on survivors' loyalty. Since they are frequently in a position to be powerful mediators of the special relationship with customers that most organizations are now seeking to develop, this may be a serious concern for these organizations.

The report adds: 'If the predicted switch of organisational emphasis to innovation, creativity and growth takes place, it suggests the need to develop qualitatively different employer/employee relationships from those derived from a simple financial management philosophy. In this case, a new relationship may be required which cannot simply be taken up where the original one left off. For the trust that underpinned working relationships before these changes took place has now been lost.'

The old implicit deal between the organization and the people it employed, points out Future Perfect, was security of employment in exchange for loyalty and commitment. There was a deep psychological contract. In fact, adds the report, this traditional concept of a career for life began to shift for individuals in the 1970s, as rapid social, economic and technological change started to encourage successive or multiple careers: 'This development began to move the concept of "career" away from the idea of advancement (in terms of position, money and status) and towards the idea of a lifelong sequence of personal experiences (perceived growth adapted to the individual's needs at his or her particular life-state).'

As discussed in Chapter Two, this implied psychological contract in large organizations – employment in small organizations was always perceived to be more risky – probably owed much to the expansion of those organizations. (Security of employment had never applied to all employees. Until the passing of the Contracts of Employment Act in 1963, hourly paid employees could be dismissed with an hour's notice, workers paid purely on piecework could be dismissed without notice. The Redundancy Payments Act, 1965, was a response to the major layoffs of 1962–3.)

'Nevertheless,' suggests Future Perfect, 'the restructuring and downsizing of the 1980s and 1990s has been perceived by those in employment as a unilateral act which has eroded dramatically the confidence of most employees in most employers. There is a substantial degree of alienation among the workforce which poses a real problem for organisations as they move towards growth.'

In seeking the basis of a new contract to replace the old, organizations should consider two main imperatives, suggests the report:

- the ability to deliver their service and products as profitably as possible, and
- the ability to renew products, services and even businesses to ensure that they can provide whatever the customer will want in future.

'The first imperative has been largely the focus of activities of the last decade,' the report adds. 'The second imperative is increasing in importance and its successful pursuit will depend on the capacity of the organisation to innovate. Innovation is most likely to flourish when there is an infusion of new ideas and new people with key skills and knowledge. Organizations are therefore likely to value high flexibility of contractual relations and seek the services of employees who are customer facing, with a specialist knowledge of the markets in which the business operates currently, and therefore able to exercise authority to take decisions quickly on behalf of the organization.'

The basis for building a robust future working relationship between organizations and employees is 'mutual interdependency', suggests Future Perfect. 'For although the delivery function of the organization may require the retention of manpower, the innovation function will not. Thus, the organization may wish to hold the balance between retention and flexibility and may wish to reserve the ability to contract with staff rather than employ them.

'This is easy to say and hard to achieve for individuals and employers, given where they start from. Substantial problems are reported in shifting from current mind-sets. The organization is often stuck in a view that its position is a powerful one in relation to its employees, that it will remain so and therefore that it does not need to change – despite the evidence being to the contrary.'

At a time when organizations are still in a buyer's market with regard to labour, they feel little pressure to change their career management policies. But, argues Future Perfect, a question for organizations to consider is whether or not they are at risk of losing key employees in future if they do not provide the proper support to ensure employability: 'The perceived risk of an approach to career management aimed at increasing the skills and options of those benefiting from them, is a felt loss of control on the part of management. Doubts are raised that such activity might undermine productivity rather than increase it. And sharing information with employees seems to offer the chance of losing much and gaining little. If the news is bad the assumption is that morale and productivity will suffer, people may abandon ship and the performance of the operation will deteriorate, hurting the company and reducing the operation's value to a potential buyer.

'But, it is argued by some commentators, the degree of control which managers have over people is evaporating in any case. In fact, tomorrow's managers may have no choice. In an age of mobility,

84

companies may face even greater dangers if they do not commit themselves to developing self-reliant workers.'

In our experience, organizations which have been brave enough to tell their employees 'bad news' have been surprised and gratified by the response. Staff may not have access to all the financial data that managers do, but they know when they are busy or when they have unsold inventory. Consequently, bad news rarely comes as a great surprise. In a number of small-scale studies, when we have asked staff what they most wanted from their managers a very common response was: 'Honesty'. Honesty was clearly interpreted by staff as including a willingness to acknowledge and confront bad news.

Offloading the wrong people

There is strong evidence to suggest that organizations are going about delayering in the wrong way and that this is having an adverse affect on career planning. Classically, organizations are offering voluntary severance. People are free to walk away. Who walks away? With any luck, some of them will be those who have reached the end of the road. They have become disenchanted with the job they are doing or are no longer in tune with the organization, in which case everyone benefits. From our analysis in Chapter Two, it is the Rocks that companies would most like to walk away. By their nature, however, they may be among those least likely to walk.

Some of those who walk away have probably become uneasy about their prospects and they take the deal on offer because they are afraid it will get worse if they stay. This is compounded by the company's willingness to offer them terms that won't entice them to stay forever. This may tip the balance, particularly for people for whom security and stability are important, who would otherwise have stayed with the organization. They will be tempted to jump ship, although the organization may not have intended them to jump. Then the organization is likely to lose some of its leaders, some of the entrepreneurial spirits who will be happy to take the money and go and work somewhere else. If it's voluntary severance, there won't necessarily be a clear-cut mechanism to hold on to them. Among those most likely to leave are our Nomads who will appreciate the organization's subsidizing their natural restlessness. Palm Trees may, under duress, uproot themselves sufficiently to search for another oasis.

Research by KPMG, the major accountancy and consulting group, indicates that companies are discovering belatedly that downsizing exercises have deprived them of the people they would most like to keep. The group surveyed six major companies which had cut on average 30 per cent of staff. Robin Linnecar, a partner of KPMG Career Consulting, observes: 'Two of the six felt very strongly that they had lost people whom they now wish they had. These were people they had let go, or who had left after becoming alienated by the way the others had been treated.'

One top company that has gone through a major programme of staff cuts admitted that it is inevitable when a firm calls for voluntary redundancies that there will be a loss of both young talent, the potential high-flyers who can easily pick up jobs elsewhere, as well as older, more experienced staff who have the financial security to retire early.

John Arnold, of Manchester School of Management comments: 'Several organizations are saying, "We overdid it: we've not only stripped out too many people; we've also lost some of the wrong people, people we should have kept." It's a perception that is gaining ground.'

He says that good people are lost not only because they put up their hands for voluntary redundancy, but also because organizations tend arbitrarily to cut out particular levels and jobs: 'Some people are simply in the wrong place at the wrong time. They might be people who should be kept and moved, but that isn't considered. It's quite common to shed people in this thoughtless way.'

As was pointed out in Chapter Four, leadership is not widely perceived as a scarce resource. When people are screened on leaving a company nobody raises any questions about how good a leader he or she is. Companies watch talent walk away. They should manage their delayering differently. They should scrutinize their people, identify those with some leadership skills and hold on to them. It is folly to encourage a scarce resource to walk out of the door.

Organizations should also give a lot more thought to the people who stay with them, how to develop those who are already emerging as leaders and how to recognize new leaders. These are key issues because if leadership is a scarce resource, ways need to be found to develop it. Organizations need to recognize the importance of spotting leadership talent, developing it, holding on to it, expanding it and trying to cope with the fact that this is a scarce resource. They should ask themselves what can be done to improve it. That means giving people development opportunities and providing coaching and mentoring and help of that kind. They should give much greater attention to helping their potential leaders to develop their interpersonal skills – their ability to influence and be influenced – and to develop their skills in changing their own and others' paradigms.

There is also the very important question of how to develop people who are not leaders. In most large organizations there are twin career tracks. One track is for the organization's high-flyers destined for the top jobs, the other for the technical experts who don't want to become general managers. What of those who are neither high-flyers nor outstanding technically or professionally? A callous solution is to treat them as the ultimately disposable workforce. Organizations could hire and fire at need, claiming that they are simply recognizing the market realities. Nobody works for an organization for ever; nobody has a permanent contract. This notion of the flexible firm attracted a great deal of attention in the 1980s, but, as Charles Handy acknowledges in his book, *The Empty Raincoat*, it doesn't work for the whole economy. If every organization relies on hiring from the market nobody ever organizes the training and development. Everyone leaves it to the market, but the market will always under-provide.

Companies don't want to pay to train people in general skills which raise the employee's productivity for all employers. For example, literacy would raise productivity in almost all jobs. As the employee's performance is enhanced in all jobs employers are reluctant to meet the training costs and then watch the employee walk away. If this happens, the employer pays the cost and the employee reaps all the benefits as they can command a higher wage for their greater productivity. If the skills are specific, on the other hand, it may be worth providing the training because they only raise productivity in that particular environment. At one level all companies provide specific training whether they want to or not: knowing who is who in the company, knowing its rules and routines, understanding the relationships, appreciating its culture and beliefs, all the intricate relationships between an organization and its clients and suppliers. All of these are specific skills and may be learned simply through experience. Other specific skills may be formally taught. For example, software systems that are unique to one company will require specific training. Companies will be most willing to invest in this training if they are convinced that employees will stay long enough for them to recoup the training costs. Unfortunately, in a world of more rapid change and greater uncertainty, the likelihood of employees staying around is reduced. Consequently, companies will only deliberately engage in those forms of training that have the highest rates of return and therefore pay back the investment as quickly as possible. At the same time, companies may have to pay their staff more generously to ensure they do not seek alternative employment. This additional cost is a further disincentive to companies to undertake training. In reality most training lies not at either extreme of general or specific but somewhere in between.

In these circumstances, what organizations are offering is greater employability in an uncertain world in return for flexibility and lower costs. What organizations can offer is not necessarily careers in their hierarchy but continuous employment with a variety of organizations because of continuously developing abilities. From the employees' perspective, they can offer much greater flexibility in return for training and development. As employees are less likely to rise in the hierarchy – because there are fewer opportunities – their earnings will not be as high. Their prospective lifetime earnings will be enhanced, however, if they can remain continuously in employment. In effect, organizations can offer more training and development in return for greater flexibility and lower costs. Some employees will be very comfortable with this trade. Others, especially those identified by Schein as having career anchors grounded in security, will find it threatening. Organizations and their temporary employees will find it difficult to change their attitudes. Organizations will miss the degree of control that lifetime employment offered; employees will miss the security they felt had been guaranteed.

Whether it is technical or managerial or professional expertise, organizations need to be creating opportunities all the time. Some of the ground rules for that have been established earlier in this book. It involves encouraging people to show a generosity of spirit. It also means urging people to work more at the leading edge. It demands that organizations challenge their people in one way or another. It means organizations must seek out clients who will really stretch and push the organization's employees, so that an environment of continuing development and progress is created.

To achieve this, organizations must create open internal markets. In the old days, people were hired to do a particular job and work in a particular function or location. That kind of inflexibility is incompatible with succeeding in today's fiercely competitive environments. Instead of adopting a hire and fire policy with the consequent loss of specific skills and the uncertainties of new recruits, organizations could construct themselves as open markets where existing employees would be encouraged to seek out new opportunities all the time. Many organizations, as a matter of routine, advertise all job vacancies internally to encourage internal movement and development. This is helpful, but it reinforces the notion that development is about whole job shifts. In reality much development occurs through additional challenges while holding down an existing job.

One useful development would be the creation of open information systems that encourage people to volunteer for project groups and similar new initiatives. Project groups, task forces, working parties – all of these are the means by which organizations come to terms with their futures. All of these *ad hoc* organizational forms provide major opportunities for personal development. Most organizations have not yet learned to see them as internal vacancies just as much as whole jobs. People are still invited to join project groups. The market for these development opportunities is closed, not open. Organizations could benefit greatly by routinely posting all such opportunities on their own e-mail systems. The information would be widely disseminated and the organization could track those who are volunteering for development. Organizations could also track those who were not volunteering and identify their Rocks before they become too embedded.

Organizations must do more than simply reveal the existence of project teams, task forces and working parties. They must indicate the extent to which individuals are able to volunteer for inclusion. They must make clear the terms of inclusion – what is expected of those joining a particular project in terms of time, effort and commitment. They must be aware of the dangers of erecting unnecessary barriers by insisting on levels of experience or qualification that disqualify all but the very few. (The very few are probably already very busy.) Who decides who may join a particular project? Is it the organization, the project leader, the project team or the individual volunteer? Is it possible for people to join on a temporary basis to find out more about what is going on?

Tools for open communication

Information technology systems provide one of the best means for achieving open communications. Electronic bulletin boards are a good example. New projects can be flagged up electronically with a brief explanation of what they aim to achieve. It makes it very easy. It doesn't have to be physically managed. It doesn't require anyone to sit around all day co-ordinating or controlling it. It provides better opportunities for people to volunteer for project groups. Keen managers will seize the opportunities. If organizations create the right kind of environment people will understand the significance of volunteering and become involved.

Electronic open-market tools create a much more decentralized and a much more flexible and responsive method of encouraging a career-resilient workforce. If managers are wondering what to do with their career and how to generate their employability, they can instantly see where the new opportunities are arising. They can relate their own skills to the new trends coming up over the horizon. They can make judgements about where they want to go next.

None of this stops the organization from hiring outside to meet specific shortages. None of this necessarily stops the organization from encouraging people to move on; but it does create more opportunities for existing employees and enables organizations to share development costs with their employees rather than paying the premium required from hiring in the open market.

Stereotype?

Career paths today no longer follow the stereotypical upward movement. It could be argued that this was never the case anyway. Most successful managers will tell you that their career paths were much more complex than that. In one organization with which we did some consulting work, a common perception by managers was that the normal career path was inside functional silos. However, every manager we interviewed described themselves as atypical because they had worked in two or more functions. When that inconsistency was fed back to the client, the initial response was incredulity until a check among all the people present confirmed our findings.

Not everyone can get to the top of the hierarchy. With a simple assumption about how long managers remain in post and the number of levels in the hierarchy, it is possible to estimate promotion probabilities. If the average manager is in a post for four years and has a forty-year working life, and the organization has ten levels in its hierarchy, the average employee has nine potential promotion opportunities. If the typical span of control is one to six, at any one time an employee has a one to six chance of taking the next job up. Each employee has a promotion probability of one in six to the power of nine of making it to the top. The odds are approximately one in ten million. Of course, promotions are not entirely random and many organizations have less than ten levels in their hierarchy. Both of these factors would improve the odds for the ambitious and the able. In many organizations the span of control is now wider than one to six which reduces the odds. Overall, the concept of continuous progression as a means of defining careers seems inconsistent with the probabilities.

Faced by these odds or the personal costs involved in obtaining successive promotions, some employees opt out, deciding it is not worth the hassle. Perhaps they would be required to spend a period abroad in some remote country, which is something they would not relish; or the next level up requires them to become embroiled in corporate politics and they are not turned on by that. There are a host of different deterrents.

That adds up to an organizational shift. Organizations need to be discouraged from what is arguably wasted effort – trying to carry out more and more manpower forecasting, which is more and more difficult to do. Instead, they should focus on managing the real time information systems about where the current pressures are, where the shortages and the developing areas are and how to make that information available to as many of their staff as possible.

The wrong values
The organizational context is important. The job itself may suit a manager very well; the effort expected by the organization could be acceptable; the career opportunities available may match the manager's needs. Despite all these advantages, the employment itself may be intolerable, perhaps because the organization's values do not match those of the individual. An individual who values autonomy will be profoundly uncomfortable in an organization that values control. An individual who values entrepreneurial creativity will be out of place in an organization that values tradition and conformity. In such cases, individuals usually recognize the incompatibility early and seek to move on. They either move or under-perform.

An organization attracts some individuals and repels others because of the values it embodies. The values it embodies are reflected in its culture. Culture reflects the organization's collective perception of the problems that it faces and appropriate means of overcoming those problems. An organization manifests its culture in many different ways. It is manifested in the reward system – in what is rewarded and how it is rewarded; in the stories and myths of the organization; in its rituals and routines; in its power relationships and in all its human resources practices and policies.

Culture is also reflected in the physical architecture of the organization. If managers are all housed in separate offices, there will be far less sharing than if they work in an open-plan environment. If office space and location reflect levels in the hierarchy, then the importance of seniority and status are made obvious. If managers really need each other's inputs in order to make things work, an open-plan environment is much more likely to create some kind of real sharing and generosity of spirit than if everyone is sitting and working with their own PC in a private office, never having the chance to talk to anybody. Organizations can physically and organizationally structure things in such a way that it makes this easier or more difficult.

Organizations that wish to signal their adoption of a more flexible approach to employment need to review their own culture to ask if it gives the right signals to those it wishes to attract or repel. Articulating a philosophy of flexibility and personal development while maintaining a culture that values seniority and functional expertise may cause considerable confusion. An organization that wishes to be more flexible must ensure that its culture offers signals that value flexibility. Openness, support for lateral moves, willingness to re-hire those who resigned and progressed, emphasis on personal development, flexibility over employment contracts – those are the marks of a flexible organization.

More personal choice

The consequences of more flexibility are as yet dimly recognized. More flexibility by employees means less control by organizations. Less control by organizations means changing roles or the elimination of roles inside the organization. If the Human Resources function has seen itself as a controller – albeit a benign controller – with its succession plans and developmental programmes and assessment centres, it now has to revise its vision of itself.

Individuals also have choices. Individuals may prefer to work for one organization rather than another – those for whom some concept of public service is very important may eschew commercial organizations. Individuals may decide that, despite the dangers of over-specialization, they wish to pursue development in a narrow area because it has great appeal for them. For all these individuals, one of the advantages of a more open market is that they have more personal choice.

Imagine a manager who would seriously like to enhance his counselling skills. He finds a college running such a course in the evenings. He goes and enhances his counselling skills. Then he starts looking for opportunities to use his new skills in his workplace. He keeps reading the open information systems and there are no appropriate opportunities. At that point he has a career choice. If he really wants to use his newly developed skills then he needs to move organizations.

The activities undertaken in working parties and task forces and project groups are tomorrow's jobs. These are the areas where organizations are trying to push back the boundaries; these are the areas where they are going to need expertise tomorrow. Working parties, task forces and project groups provide a ready snapshot about developing trends. Managers can take a view about whether or not they want to invest their time and energy and development in any of these. If they do not, they risk reducing their employability. The choice rests with individual managers.

If they decide to focus on a narrow segment because it suits them, that is their choice. If they try to cover too wide a range, they may not acquire the depth of expertise which is needed to carry them forward, but that may be acceptable to those individuals. For the organization, it means opening up the options and no longer trying to manage so rigidly.

Most organizations understand the notion of job-posting. Many of them have developed it to a high level. No jobs are advertised externally until they're advertised internally. That was appropriate when a career meant a lifetime with one organization. These days, they ought to go a step beyond that, because job-posting is too limited and too rigid.

Imagine a manager who has always worked in production. She would like to move to marketing. In the conventional approach to career planning, the prospect of making such a major career switch is very remote. But suppose there was some kind of working party with marketing responsibility that needed someone with a production background on the team. She might offer to work on that. Then as she begins to understand how marketing people operate, she would be clearer about whether it is truly something she wants to take up. The experience might, on the other hand, leave her feeling that they are not the sort of people with whom she is comfortable working. It would also be a chance for the marketers to take a look at her and decide whether her contribution was professional and really useful. If so, they might well call on her services again. It's all about trying to free up the system.

However, it's not about doing it all through the HR function. The role of the HR function moves from central planning and command to fostering an efficient internal market. There is a role in setting standards and clarifying contractual obligations, but the decisions are made by the parties most directly involved. It's about creating more open systems so that people can find out what's going on and begin to volunteer their involvement. That probably means there would have to be some kind of exclusion mechanism. That might mean some of the members of the task force are appointed to accept or reject applicants. This creates a lot of healthy dynamism in terms of people bringing in those who appear to be like-minded and the kind of people they can work with. That is an enlightened way for organizations to create career opportunities for people.

Introducing career management

Judith Mills, director of programmes at London-based Management Career Development (MCD), warns that career management needs to be introduced with great care: 'Many employees have been unsettled by the events of the last few years and are cautious about many aspects of their lives. For a career management programme to be successful, it is key for the introducers to explain fully the reason for the programme and the anticipated outcomes.'

Unless handled cautiously, individuals may become suspicious and defensive, perhaps believing it is just the first tentative step towards redundancy and outplacement, Mills suggests. Career management that emphasizes an open market, individual learning and development opportunities is valid and has a role to play.

This is especially true when a company has recently undergone a major redundancy or outplacement programme. Drake Beam Morin

94

(DBM) recently commissioned a report into what it describes as 'survivor syndrome'. According to the study, there is a lot of uncertainty among the staff who survive such an exercise and a feeling of insecurity that tends to outweigh any possible euphoria generated from escaping their worst fears.

Peter Trigg, chairman of DBM's UK division, explains: 'Despite the reported upturn in the economy, many organizations are still having to restructure, forcing staff redundancies. Unless the employer is geared up to change, the surviving employees can find they are being asked to work twice as hard to compensate for lost personnel. They may also feel very guilty about losing friends and colleagues, which leads to low morale, reduced productivity, and even resignation. Major organizations must make efforts to regain employee trust and commitment if they are to avoid survivor syndrome taking its toll on profits.'

John Crace, writing in *The Sunday Times* (12 February 1995), acknowledges that trying to win back employee loyalty after a sustained period of recession and layoffs is no easy task: 'Given that the employees' psychological contract whereby loyalty and hard work are rewarded by job security is a thing of the past and that the emerging trends are for multiple career changes and fewer promotional opportunities, it is not easy for employers to ensure the well-being and commitment of their surviving workforce.'

To offset the problem, Crace suggests that two requirements must be met. The first is that management should acknowledge the full impact of the transition survivors are likely to be undergoing and give them a sense of direction and vision. The second is that the types of relationship, both formal and implicit, that the organization wishes to have with its employees should be redefined.

A positive career management programme can help to restore trust and faith in future prospects if handled properly, maintains Judith Mills: 'Once people understand the contents and meet the providers of the new programme, trust, involvement and commitment can be built up. Career management initiatives which have "front end" consultation and information have a far greater chance of take-up and success. Simply "signing up" employees to programmes so that subsequent changes or decisions can be managed in the workplace is not effective in today's working environment. Line managers should also be fully briefed on the programme and ideally undertake it before themselves.'

Mills suggests that following downsizing and restructuring, career management programmes can be used to send employees messages that they are valued by the organization and their commitment is essential to the company's future success. Blanket programmes involving all staff can work – career management is not just for star performers. A productivity lift throughout the organization is often experienced following such a programme. A momentum is created, partly due to participants talking to one another more readily about themselves, their experience with others and partly because they can see where their efforts fit into the whole. She adds: 'Suspicions can be aroused when programmes are targeted at certain levels within an organization. Care should be taken to establish the need for the programme in the first place; it could be as a result of redundancy, restructuring, management changes; all affect career paths and opportunities. Getting implementation right is paramount. If not tackled effectively, the flipside – poor career management – could come about: increased turnover, poor appointments, inappropriate job applications, disenchantment and increased numbers of poor performers.'

Mills lists the following as the most favoured methods of implementing career management within organizations:

- Career management workshops, seminars and training programmes
- Personal career assessment (often using psychometrics), counselling, coaching and mentoring programmes
- Working with resources from career development centres, e.g. self-paced learning programmes, computerized career packages, self-assessment tools and workbooks.

She adds: 'Ultimately it is line managers who are being expected to go beyond their traditional role and become personal and performance appraisers, career advisers, coaches, mentors and identifiers of development needs. This role may be in addition to new-found responsibilities for recruitment and career succession planning inherited from HR. Ironically, often the last thing they are doing is managing their own careers!

'Many managers are daunted by the prospect of being all things to their employees. Those who perceive themselves as task managers want to "get the job done"; if there's time left they will spend this with staff, thus providing them with the support, guidance and counsel needed to help them manage their careers effectively. People need support to make sense of the changes they have been through and develop new skills so they are equipped for future challenges.'

It is in their own interest for companies to introduce well-designed career management programmes. The benefits to the organization can be significant, in Mills' opinion:

- More highly motivated and loyal workforce
- Creation of an internal job market
- Employees know where they 'fit' in the organization
- Less external recruitment and related cost savings
- A positive response to equal opportunities legislation
- Decreased employee turnover
- Increased productivity

She says: 'As with much personal development, it is difficult to provide hard factual evidence of success. However, the "feel good" factor improves, people are less stressed, more focused and better able to cope with change.

'Career management is an effective way for individuals to realize their potential and identify and achieve their goals. It helps organizations to retain staff and indeed the provision of career management opportunities in US organizations such as Sun Microsystems is seen by job hunters as added value, thus easing recruitment difficulties. It also allows people to develop long-term careers, primarily within the organization. Successful career planning produces a win-win situation: committed organizations with loyal, motivated staff.'

Double talk

There are still many companies, however, whose actions are a long way from this idealistic view of care and support for managers trying to find new career paths in the flattened pyramid. John O'Brien, the London-based career counsellor, doesn't like a lot of what he finds in the corporate jungle: 'There's an awful dilemma at the moment, because the better companies have this stated belief – often in their mission statement – about the importance of people. However, what it comes down to at the end of the day is actual performance and it tends to be very short-term.

'I don't want to name companies, but the chief executive of one particular huge organization takes the view basically: we will work them into the ground, we'll get what we can out of them and then we'll chuck some money at them and we'll chuck them out. That to me is not empowerment or job enrichment. It's abuse.

'Even in companies that claim to have all these development programmes, there's still this double talk in terms of what they're actually about. I see many people for counselling and career change and in transition or outplacement and I think most people have lost confidence to a very high degree in their organizations. They no longer have any trust. It used to be a job for life. That's gone, but the hours people put in are incredibly long. I think there's very often a total imbalance in people's lives. I have people saying to me: "You're absolutely right. My wife's been saying to me for years that I've changed. I'm not the person she married. Now that I stand back and look at it, I don't know how I got here." These are people who have really become political animals in an organization, clawing their way to the top, working all the hours that God sends them, neglecting their families, their children and still ending up being discarded on the scrap heap. That's an awful picture to paint.'

A growth market

Advising companies on how to help their managers organize their careers in the age of the flattened pyramid promises to be a huge growth market for consulting firms. The first consultancies to realize the potential are the outplacement agencies which have traditionally used career planning as part of their counselling for redundant managers. Drake Beam Morin claims to be the biggest outplacement and career management consultancy in the world and it has not been slow to recognize the new opportunities, applying such techniques as questionnaires based on Edgar Schein's career anchors theory. Says Peter Trigg, managing director of DBM's London office: 'Somebody has to map out the individual's career and we say the good company should do it. We have programmes for that which say: Are you happy in your work? Where would you really like to be? If you can't achieve that and you think that's where you ought to be, there's some sort of dysfunction somewhere.'

Traditionally, in most companies such intense introspection was only carried out – if ever – during an outplacement programme, but there is growing realization that this is often closing the stable door after the horse has bolted. Trigg adds: 'Good companies have got rid of all the people generally they feel they can get rid of and there's a lot of talk now as to whether it really achieved the objectives. We say that's because it wasn't properly planned, because if you do plan it properly you should get the benefits. What companies are now saying is that they want the workforce they have left to be the best trained and the most loyal workforce they can get in the new circumstances. How do they achieve that? They achieve it really by having some sort of career path discussions with the individuals to show interest in them and also to get them to consider and take on board their own responsibility for developing themselves.'

The survival syndrome – the uncertainty, guilt and disorientation that those who have survived a major redundancy programme feel – makes corporate career management all the more urgent, in Trigg's view: 'Those who are left find themselves working much harder. You frequently see the scenario that someone who is still in the company has heard that Jim got a payoff, is working for himself or whatever, and here he or she is, still in the company with a frozen salary and doing his or her job and everyone else's – and uncertain whether he or she is still going to be there tomorrow.

'I have to say that the theory of career management is better than the practice, but I see it as a big market provided we can get it right – and of course a good contributor to society and the country at large. There are issues about how often it should be done. Should it be like a 10,000-mile service? It ought to be more than that. I think enlightened companies are doing it well. I do think the better companies are striving – in difficult times I must say – for some sort of equitable process whereby people can know what they want to do and what they've got to do to get there. They are encouraging them to take charge of their careers.'

The obvious fact revealed by Trigg's comments is that many companies are still hoping for loyalty from their employees despite the fact that experience has taught staff that loyalty is a one-way option. Such companies have not yet come to terms with the need to find a new basis for their relationship with their staff. If mutual loyalty is no longer available, then organizations need to find a new basis for mutual benefit.

Continuous learning
There is also encouragement coming from the Institute of Management which, in September 1995, launched a continuing professional

development (CPD) initiative to persuade individuals to take charge of their own development. Announcing the initiative, the IM declared that 'with the demise of the job for life, CPD places responsibility for development on individuals. Flexibility and responsiveness to individual needs are the key elements of the CPD policy.' The IM added: 'Managers wishing to ensure their employability can no longer rely on a degree or professional qualification obtained at the outset of their careers.'

Michael Heseltine, deputy prime minister and first secretary of state, commenting on the new policy, said: 'In a world where the rate of change is ever increasing, training throughout working life is now essential both for individuals and for the UK's competitiveness. The CPD initiative provides an excellent framework for ensuring that managers are able to keep their skills up-to-date.'

The IM believes that individuals must continually develop their skills so that the UK can remain competitive in world markets. It urges employers to facilitate training and give managers opportunities to work in a range of the organization's activities. It also urges the government to enhance incentive schemes to encourage individuals to invest in their own development.

The IM's policy differs from that of other professional institutions because it does not merely accumulate 'CPD points' for attending courses. Course attendance does not necessarily demonstrate development; it provides no evidence of improved competency or increased knowledge. A wide range of developmental activities need to be undertaken to satisfy individual needs. Different career stages, argues the IM, will demand different mixes of activities. These will include courses, but informal and on-the-job activities are often equally effective. The content and pace of the development can only be decided by individuals, often in conjunction with their employers.

In the opinion of Roger Young, IM director general: 'For managers to survive in today's changing employment market, they must maintain their employability. Skills constantly need to be updated and improved. Individuals must be prepared to invest in their own development. CPD is all about the practice of maintaining one's professional development throughout a career and considering that you never have sufficient skill or knowledge. All new members of the Institute commit themselves to this policy when they join.

'Our aim is to enhance the ability of managers to achieve results.

They need to obtain personal satisfaction from their work and so contribute to the success of their organization. This in turn will strengthen the UK's economic and competitive performance.'

Judith Mills believes managers will be more inclined to review their careers regularly when the mystique is removed from the whole process: 'People do an annual audit of their financials and have regular health checks, but they don't do it with their careers, which is a bit daft. Maybe people don't manage their careers because people like myself make it too complicated.'

To simplify the process, Mills has developed a career audit model based on an uncomplicated definition to career management: 'to understand your career and the part it plays in your life.' She adds: 'My experience is that people are working so hard and keeping their heads down that they have forgotten to understand the significance of what they are doing. They need some outside counselling to help them get some sense of where their needs merge with the organization.'

Encouraging managers to review where their needs and those of their organizations coincide and conflict is obviously valuable, although it is a brave and caring organization that is willing to fund such an open review. The other issue concerns what the organizations are trying to accomplish. By demanding more and more from managers while offering less seems short-sighted. In part, it reflects the influence of the greater rewards now for very senior executives. Just as many people buy lottery tickets although they know that the odds on winning are very low, the lure is the possibility of securing a major prize. When more and more managers realize just how long the odds are – and their own experience will be a useful guide – organizations will be forced into a radical reappraisal of the offer they make their managers. A remote chance of a big prize may be replaced by greater opportunities to secure employability and achieve a better balance between work and other activities and pastimes.

A climate of open communication

Judith Mills does not believe career management can work in organizations that do not have an appropriate corporate culture. There needs to be a climate of open communication, 'because if you're talking about career management you're actually saying that you are prepared as an organization to have an adult conversation with somebody about their career. Individuals have got to bare their souls in terms of what they want, but the organization has to be able to handle that and have a good knowledge of what the opportunities are and what the culture is – to work in partnership.'

The wrong approach, in Mills' view, is typified by the organization that turns down a manager's application to tackle a new project because he or she does not appear to have the necessary qualifications. Organizations should now be encouraging managers to take risks with their careers and provide the coaching and counselling to help them make judgements about what is possible and what isn't.

In the model Mills has developed to help managers, she first of all asks them to examine how they arrived at their current position and how their work and personal life are interrelated. They focus on their past successes and identify the moments when they most enjoyed their work. What was the nature of the work? What sort of people were they working with? As part of the exercise participants are asked to make a list of their fifty top achievements. The emphasis is on the positive aspects of their life rather than their weaknesses.

The next stage of the exercise is to persuade managers to accept the reality of their present situation, using such techniques as a SWOT analysis. The third part involves persuading the participants to take responsibility for their future. They have to decide what they want from their careers and how they are going to go about getting there. Mills says: 'Quite a lot of people have barriers to achieving what they want from their careers. What stops them from wanting things? What are the old scripts and what do they need to let go?'

There is a lot of theory about what organizations should be doing to take account of the shift in career patterns, but translating that into action is proving a serious problem. Mills believes there are a number of reasons for this: 'I don't think some organizations know what to do. In the past few years they have really been in high control. They had to be to take care of the bottom line. So organizations have gone into quite a telling mode, whereas if you're talking about career management it is a question of going back into the coaching mode again. It is quite a shift. There is also the jargon about the new "psychological contract". Now that an organization can't offer a job for life, what should it be offering? The simple answer is encouragement to people to keep up-dating their skills.

'There is also talk about "psychic income", that people come to work for a lot of things other than money, which is something we seem to have lost sight of. The concept is terribly old-fashioned –

going back to Maslow – but there is an element in it that people do want something else out of work.'

At the other end of the scale, some companies in the US have pushed forward the frontiers of career management and opened up new dimensions. The pioneers include Apple Computer, Rachem Corporation, a manufacturer of specialized industrial products and 3Com Corporation, a maker of computer networking products. Not surprisingly, many of these companies are located in Silicon Valley, where the challenge of coping with the ever-faster pace of change has long been a way of life. Another of the pioneers is Sun Microsystems, the California-based work station manufacturer, which has introduced the concept of career centres (see Chapter Seven). The US computer company actually encourages people to leave the organization temporarily and seek experience with other companies to help their career progression. Sun Microsystems takes the enlightened view that managers who have benefited from this broadening experience will return to the company far better equipped to develop their careers and enhance their roles.

Barriers to employability
The widely advocated notion of employability as a panacea to the impact of change on career planning is as yet unproven. Experts at Ashridge Management College suggest that the world of employability is unlikely to materialize fully until companies have tackled the fundamental changes in grading and reward systems required to make leaner, flatter managers. The authors (Laurence Handy, Viki Holton and Peter James) of an article in the April 1995 issue of the Ashridge journal, *directions*, argue that current systems too often:

- focus on individual performance when contribution to teams may be the more significant issue
- couple rewards to promotions even though these are becoming less frequent
- direct attention to pay and cars when individuals may be more interested in non-material benefits.

The authors add: 'One challenge is therefore to find more effective ways of identifying and assessing team contributions. This can be done either by inputs – so that people are rewarded for team-working skills – or through outputs, with team rewards which are shared between members. Competency schemes and 360-degree feedback are valuable supports for the former and clear team objectives and performance criteria for the latter. American Express is one company which is moving in this direction with over 10,000 of its staff now participating in team incentive programmes.'

The authors of the article from the *Harvard Business Review* mentioned in Chapter 5 raised a number of critical issues that arise from taking the employability route. In the article, 'Toward a Career-Resilient Workforce', Robert H. Waterman, Jr, Judith A. Waterman and Betsy A. Collard, observe: 'Some management thinkers are arguing that instead of the traditional focus on *employment*, the focus should now be on *employability*. In other words, we should forget about clinging desperately to one job, one company or one career path. What matters now is having the competitive skills required to find work when we need it, wherever we can find it.'

This, suggests the authors, poses some fundamental questions for organizations: What responsibility, if any, does a company now have to employees? Ought management to be concerned only about staying lean to keep up with competition and not about acting mean? Should management be satisfied with employees whose only loyalty is to their own careers? How can an enterprise build capabilities, forge empowered teams, develop a deep understanding of its customers, and – most important – create a sense of community or common purpose, unless it has a relationship with its employees based on mutual trust and caring? And how can an enterprise build such a relationship unless it commits something to employees and employees commit something to it?

The answer, maintain the authors, is by 'entering into a new covenant under which the employer and the employee share responsibility for maintaining – even enhancing – the individual's employability inside *and outside* the company. Under the old covenant, employees entrusted major decisions affecting their careers to a parental organization. Often, the result was a dependent employee and a relatively static workforce, with a set of static skills. Under the new covenant, employers give individuals the opportunity to develop greatly enhanced employability in exchange for better productivity and some degree of commitment to company purpose and community for as long as the employee works there.'

It is the company's responsibility, suggest the authors, to provide employees with the tools, the open environment, and the opportunities for assessing and developing their skills; and it is the responsibility of managers at all levels to show that they care about their employees whether or not they stay with the company. The result is a 'career-resilient workforce' and a company that can thrive in an era in which the skills needed to remain competitive are changing at a dizzying pace.

What the authors mean by a career-resilient workforce is a group of employees who are not only dedicated to the idea of continuous learning but also stand ready to re-invent themselves to keep pace with change; who take responsibility for their own career management; and, last, who are committed to the company's success. For each individual, this means staying knowledgeable about market trends and understanding the skills and behaviours the company will need down the road.

Keith Faulkner, of Manpower, was one of the speakers at a forum of over 140 senior executives, held at the Royal Society of Arts in London to examine the changing relationship between employer and employee. He believes that loyalty and commitment have totally different meanings in the modern organization and argues that properly trained employees who genuinely see their employers as customers will have all the commitment already exhibited by self-employed people anxious to hold on to their clientele.

Commitment, Faulkner suggests, needs to be redefined. It can no longer be the exchange of mutual lifelong loyalty but the commitment of self-employed business ownership. If you own the services, skills and resources you have to offer an employer and are paid on the basis of what you deliver, you are potentially more committed to delivering a quality result than traditional employees who may feel they can coast and still retain a job.

Learning the lesson
There is evidence that companies are beginning to realize that they need to retain their leadership talent if they are to survive in today's highly competitive markets. The indiscriminate blood-letting that has occurred in downsizing exercises has left many organizations ill-equipped to face the future. They are beginning to learn the

lesson. John Arnold, of Manchester School of Management, says: 'Some companies are so thinned out they lack the capacity to respond quickly to new opportunities. Another fact that has emerged is that you stifle innovation when you make employees insecure. They stop taking risks. Companies that rely on innovation in products and marketing are realizing they are blocking those people with innovative potential.'

Arnold believes that this has led to a change in management attitudes: 'A number of companies are beginning to say that their people are their competitive advantage. They realize that if they want to get the best out of people they have to offer security and commitment. In return, they expect employees to be flexible about the kind of work they do, and be able to do work that requires different ranges of skills – because that's part of an organization's ability to respond to change.'

KPMG's research reveals that companies are trying to create a new culture: one that will allow them to retain the people they need, but, according to Robin Linnecar, they haven't yet figured out how to do it: 'They are trying lots of things – staff development networks, feedback sessions, advertising jobs internally first, more employee assistance programmes – but who can say if it all works?'

Arnold agrees: 'It's not clear yet whether the organizations that are doing all these things are succeeding in walking a tightrope between their own and their employees' interests. The jury is still out.'

Again, these comments reveal the dichotomy that organizations are confronted by but are not facing. If employees are treated as disposable assets to be dismissed because the organization had failed to generate sufficient demand for their services, then expecting loyalty and commitment is unrealistic. Offering lifetime employment is only a viable policy if it can be sustained. Rover have offered lifetime employment security – but have insisted that it carries no guarantees of work in a particular job or function or location. In some instances, employees who are no longer required in white-collar jobs have been reassigned to production jobs. How many employees are really prepared to be so flexible? How many organizations could countenance such mobility?

Matching the needs of self-fulfilment
An MBA dissertation by Jeremy Ebdon at Surrey European Management School at The University of Surrey provides positive

evidence that initiatives to offset the adverse effects of delayering can be beneficial. His report, *Career Development within Flat Pyramid Organisations*, attempts to assess the human consequences of the increasing propensity of organizations to delayer their structures in order to remain competitive.

He points out that much of the existing management theory about career development stresses that organizations should match the individual's needs for self-fulfilment. However, many of the criteria for this matching process are removed by delayering: people no longer have a job for life; traditional patterns of career development are implicitly limited within flat structures; feelings of job security are eroded.

The challenge to the human resource area, Ebdon suggests, is to mediate this potentially damaging process for the good of employees and the organization. His research, using data provided by the Institute of Personnel Development, sought first to assess whether organization structure affects an individual's ability to achieve self-fulfilment, and then to assess any causal link between companies' career development programmes and the level of individual self-fulfilment.

The results of the study were inconclusive. However, two broad generalizations emerged. There was no significant link between type of organization structure and the individuals' level of self-fulfilment as exhibited by staff turnover and morale. Nevertheless, there is a statistically significant link between the emphasis organizations place on career development as exhibited by such initiatives as job enrichment, personal career planning, and the levels of staff self-fulfilment as exhibited by turnover and morale.

The clear conclusion is that irrespective of structure, organizations which wish to get more from their staff must do something – and the more the better – about their staff's feelings towards their career development prospects. Companies which engage in holistic career development initiatives report lower staff turnover and higher morale.

An employment revolution
A reported shift in employer/employee relations in the US could presage a similar trend in the UK and Europe. John Epperheimer, director of corporate programs at the Career Action Center in California, refers to a new employment revolution occurring in

the US workplace. Writing in the September–October 1995 issue of *Career Action Connections*, he says: 'This time it is driven by the workers, not the employers. As the economy rebounds from years of downsizing and restructuring, workers suddenly have options again; hiring is booming compared to the same time last year. Increasingly, workers are changing their focus from merely being employed (a tall enough order in recent years) to figuring out how to make a living doing what they enjoy.'

The result, Epperheimer maintains, is that managers are confronted by employees demanding help in managing their careers: 'No longer is merely offering employment enough to retain key performers. There is a need expressed for "psychic reward". I believe this is a systematic shift that will fundamentally change how companies deal with their workers.

'Whether the opportunity to search for meaningful work comes from being bounced out of a job or from choosing to sell your skills as an independent contractor because it offers more freedom, American companies have unleashed a new monster that will not go back into its cage. The worker with an independent attitude is the new 600-pound gorilla of the workplace.'

Epperheimer argues that the new attitude was forced on workers by the organizations that employ them: 'With an eye mostly on quarterly earnings, companies began to use layoffs as a way to cut expenses. Re-engineering led to the elimination of thousands of positions. Companies have discarded job guarantees and chain-of-command structures that controlled workers. They have replaced them with free-agency, team-style management, continuous change and faster and faster product life cycles. Today, nobody's job is safe. Now, however, companies must focus on how to retain their most valuable core employees.'

The need for continuous learning to stay competitive in the job market, Epperheimer adds, is sinking into the heads of people who have seen their jobs or those of their friends and family evaporate in a reorganization. 'Deprived of job security, workers are responding by seeking ways to take control of their careers. From the individual's point of view the new employer-employee contract looks like this: "If the company says it can't take care of me any more, but still wants me to work long, hard hours, the least it can do is give me access to learning and training opportunities and help me to learn how to manage my career myself."'

The Career Action Center, a non-profit organization based in Palo Alto, is ideally suited to help this process. It is recognized throughout the US for its leadership and expertise in the development and delivery of career management services. It has over 8,000 individual members and has been helping people explore opportunities and make informed choices about life-work for over twenty-one years. In addition to an extensive resource library, it helps members to identify appropriate counselling programmes and to choose from a host of available workshops. These range from self-assessment, exploring career options and determining your focus, to marketing yourself and work strategies and ongoing career management.

The new avengers

If an article written by Simon Caulkin in the November issue of *Management Today* is to be believed, organizations do not have long to get their act together and to forge a new relationship with their employees. The article, alarmingly entitled 'The New Avengers', claims that a new breed of employees is emerging in a reaction to the ruthless cost-cutting measures introduced by companies in the wake of the recession. Caulkin argues that as loyalty is no longer rewarded, individuals are taking charge of their own destinies and with the breakdown of the old employment relationships, 'Me plc' has become the latest catchword. He suggests: 'As surely as Clint Eastwood returning to avenge the past, the enforcers of Me plc are calling in a debt. Years of corporate lip-service to the importance of people are finally catching up. Payment is now due in full, and in kind: for once you have rationalized and re-organized everything else, people really are the only asset.'

He adds: 'Put brutally, individuals are asking themselves: if the company no longer represents a career, a pension or "a safe job", what am I doing here? If the organization can't provide a satisfactory answer to this existential question – if it hasn't found a new bonding agent to replace the deferred gratification of the next job or a secure old age – it will fall apart at the first touch of pressure.'

Caulkin is not convinced that employability is going to provide organizations with the escape route they are anxiously seeking: 'The idea of a new contract based not on employment security but on employer-aided self-development (an adult-adult relationship rather than the parent-child relationship of the past), has obvious attractions for employers. But on closer inspection it's not clear how much this desire for a happy ending is shared by employees.

'For a start, only a minority of managers are psychologically ready to accept the reality of the arm's length employment relationships.'

He cites recent research by GHN, the career counselling consultancy, that revealed that most of the polled managers clung to the belief that their organizations were committed to their development and career despite explicit declarations to the contrary. Although nearly half were aware of the precariousness of their jobs, they were totally unprepared to take charge of their careers. Only 11 per cent had plans for self-development, 12 per cent the information to construct a CV and just 19 per cent bothered to take up company courses in professional and management skills.

Caulkin warns: 'Employers should beware. Just when the terms of trade in employment seemed most in their favour, the balance is beginning to shift back towards the individual. Straws in the wind: employment researchers are already signalling skills shortages in some areas, and the buzz on the milk-round grapevine is that companies which aren't explicitly offering development opportunities aren't getting recruits. More of a haystack than a straw is the current turmoil in pay systems, always a sensitive indicator of changing climate. As job boundaries blur, traditional pay grading systems are breaking down too.'

This paints a bleak picture and one that should send shivers down the spines of organizations that have survived the recession and thought there was reason to be optimistic about future employment conditions. But the saving grace for organizations is that ultimately it is in the interests of both employers and employees to carve out a formula that meets their mutual needs and secures future success for both parties. An ongoing war between organizations and employees would ultimately be self-defeating for both sides. For organizations the challenge is to meet the needs of those employees with the most 'attitude' who are frequently among the brightest and the best. Individuals with lesser talents may accept what the company offers. But are employees with lesser talents what the company wants?

In the following chapters, case studies illustrate the various ways companies are trying to match business goals with the career aspirations of their staff. Most would agree that they are still at the experimental stage. They are trying a whole range of innovative approaches, from using core competencies to align management skills with the prime needs of the organization, to 'lateral progression'. Only time will tell if these new approaches are going to work, but one thing all the experimenting companies have in common is the knowledge that if they don't seek out ways to retain their leadership talent they will have very little chance of surviving well into the next century.

Chapter Seven
Matching Personal Career Ambitions with Corporate Goals

One of the most significant findings to emerge from the study by Future Perfect into the impact of delayering was a shift away from *career development* towards *career planning*. Future Perfect observes that in the old, stable world of organizational certainty, career development meant providing the skills and experience to prepare for known paths, and that the task of appraisal was to assess the readiness of an individual for the next stage in his or her career. The report says: 'Under this scenario succession planning could make good sense since there was a high degree of predictability about the needs of the future. However, the 1990s have been described as an age of perhaps unprecedented uncertainty – so other models of career development are being created in which preparation supports the development of flexibility and adaptability of the individual for moves which are likely to be sideways rather than up. The vertical career appears to be giving way to the lattice career as layers of management disappear.'

The main thrust of the Future Perfect study was on careers within organizations, but as companies take on board the likely short-term nature of future employment contracts, the consultancy argues that the emphasis may move from purely career development towards career planning, where the objective may be to prepare individuals for the wider job market – and for life beyond the first career. The report comments: 'Although the personal preparation may be similar, the difference is that the purpose of fitting [employees] for outside [employment] becomes explicit and provision is created to help the individual plan for this. Career development and career planning may be seen as a continuum, and an indicator of where organizations currently stand on this continuum may be where they put the emphasis on responsibility for career development.'

Future Perfect illustrates this theory by providing examples from its survey of the different positions observed on the continuum. The consultancy stresses that no judgements are implied by the examples, since there is considerable variability in the level of uncertainty in different operating environments. What is apparent, however, is that public sector organizations in the study stand at one end of the continuum. Their staff saw the organization as being responsible for determining their careers and it was noticeable that morale and motivation were deteriorating as the opportunities for advancement disappeared. Most private sector companies in the survey saw responsibility for career development at least as joint responsibility, for the emphasis was on developing abilities for the future within the organization. However, some companies were beginning to support career planning with an acknowledgement that this could involve preparation for a move outside in due course.

The following were examples of the differing organizational positions on the career development/career planning continuum identified by Future Perfect:

- *Organization A* is facing substantial downsizing and seems to take the view that this will not involve substantial change in the nature of the work to be undertaken by the organization. Individuals within it perceive career development as a matter for the organization and see it as essentially preparation, assessment and appraisal for vertical promotion within the organization. Although it is recognized there may be some scope for short-term contracts there is as yet no real emphasis on the acquisition of new skills and competencies.

- *Organization B* is developing a group language about the competencies needed in the various roles within the organization and wants to apply these across its different businesses to ensure common standards and performance. Its intention is to develop its people for both vertical and lateral career movement. Self-development is being encouraged and a comprehensive performance management process, including formal career review, is about to be introduced.

- *Organization C* is placing greater responsibility for career development on the individual. There is more emphasis on assessment of individual needs, and on personal planning. Competencies are identified and work is in train to integrate self-assessment materials, the appraisal process and personal development planning.

- *Organization D* has a well-developed programme for career development which provides for the creation and implementation of personal development plans. It has a skills management programme in which people are assessed against a range of roles and developed accordingly. There is an explicit policy of developing lateral careers within the organization.

- *Organization E* aims to implement and achieve both general and specific competence development across the organization with a full programme of support. Personal and career development are seen as a shared responsibility. The annual appraisal process is the vehicle through which a person's uncertain future is reviewed, areas for development identified and a plan of action agreed. A current weakness identified is the lack of easy transfer to posts nationally and internationally – the systems are as yet unavailable to do this readily.

- *Organization F* puts great emphasis on personal development through a structured development programme which is a joint initiative with the trade union. Under this programme any employee may take up a course in a subject of their choice with a grant towards the cost from the company. Take-up is at the level of 30 per cent per annum. This provision supports detailed individual career plans. Regular reviews of career are held for those on the fast track.

- *Organization G* has a highly developed programme of career development. Every employee (from a total of 36,000) is offered the opportunity to participate in a personal programme of development and review. The purpose is to give the employee opportunities to identify career development aspirations, the skills required and, with management support, to create a plan of action to achieve this. Access is available to a wide range of skills development programmes run within the company and to external courses (up to MBA) organized by the company. Like Company F, a grant is available to each employee for a personal development programme, in which development is defined in very wide terms indeed. For senior staff the programme is supported by a range of executive development centres.

Within Company G the purpose of this provision is quite explicitly to develop a committed and flexible workforce. However, the company acknowledges and accepts as positive that this investment by them fits people for opportunities outside the organization, which some may well take up. Indeed, there is an informal career planning process available to all staff.

There is considerable effort on the part of the surveyed companies going into career development, but there is little evidence of career planning at the earlier stages of a career, leading to the conclusion that 'signs of a move towards a new deal in place of the old one are still fairly thin on the ground.' The survey report adds: 'There is some leading-edge activity on investment in personal development by one or two companies in this survey and an open-minded attitude on the part of both management and staff in them as to the form in which the future relationship may develop. We have little doubt that the very substantial investment that such companies are making will convert into competitive advantage for them, for we observed very high levels of management and staff commitment to, and belief in, the future of the organization.'

Future Perfect identifies three basic conditions for growing a new relationship:

a. that mutual expectations between organizations and individuals are more openly expressed.

b. that information is shared on plans, opportunities and scenarios so that neither employer nor employee are disadvantaged by being unnecessarily in the dark. (One of the surveyed organizations spent a total of 26,500 man days in explaining to a workforce of 36,000 its positions and its plans – creating opportunities for open discussion on these between staff and their local managers.)

c. that the organization's declared role shifts from being responsible for an employee's career towards being in support of the individual as he/she takes charge themselves. This means both providing resources and supporting open communication. Career management requires very open and honest communication, for it is through communication about expectations, outlook, markets and support available, that a new relationship of trust may be built. In exchange for a commitment of this kind by the organization to the individual's career interests, an equivalent commitment from the individuals may be expected. Thus each partner may develop an interest in improving the other's competitive position.

Looking at the respective roles and responsibilities of the organization and the individual in this new partnership, Future Perfect advocates that: 'The employer and the employee share responsibility for maintaining – even enhancing – the individual's employability inside and outside the company. The company may therefore need to help people to explore the job opportunities inside and out, and may facilitate life-long learning and a blame-free exit at the point the individual decides to exercise an option to pursue interests elsewhere.

'For their part, employees may need to become dedicated to the idea of continuous learning and stand ready to re-invent themselves to keep pace with change. This may mean taking over responsibility for their own career management and being committed to the company's success.'

How ready are organizations and individuals generally to strike this new deal? That is a key question. The Future Perfect survey concluded that: 'Although the new working scenario is becoming one of much more temporary employment relationships in which mutual expectations between individuals and organizations are more openly expressed, recent evidence has demonstrated that managers base their beliefs about their future careers upon their previous career history rather than upon a realistic appreciation of the present internal and external labour market conditions. In such a situation there is a need for organizations and employees to be clear and explicit about job opportunities and career preferences. Mutual satisatisfaction is likely to be achieved if the organization is truthful about opportunities and even about its inability to predict with any certainty what these will be.'

Indications are that even those organizations who are tackling the issue are at a fairly early stage in translating any of the theories into practice: 'Employees have to become responsible for their own careers, yet few have taken the notion to heart. For it is difficult to revise generations of conditioning. We all entered the workplace with expectations of career ladders and promotions and our culture has glamorized the climb to the top. Successful careers have always been built on the notion of advancement and this now changes. Further, employees – particularly those in industries hard hit by the recession – are distrustful and nervous about any corporate initiative that may make more demands on them. Older workers are especially resistant to the notion of career management.

'This implies that the process may take a long time. It also implies that it is extremely important to achieve the required shift in mind-set. Organizational support to the individual may be critical in achieving this. It is clearly in the organization's interest to invest in this way because the potential prize that awaits is access to a group of self-confident and highly competent knowledge workers able to work with the organization as it changes, and at very high levels of commitment – levels which were unusual in the traditional form of organization, in which the definition of the job tended to constrain creativity.'

A measure of the scale of the gap between organizations and their employees was provided recently by a client organization. As part of a career management review, the organization asked focus groups of its employees to list the promises that they felt the company had made when they joined. The results were lists with hundreds of items. The same groups were then asked what they had promised to the company when they joined. The result was some very short lists – some groups failed to identify a single promise that they felt they had made.

CASE STUDY: SmithKline Beecham

'The best career advice you get is usually when you are made redundant. That's normally the first time somebody actually sits down with you and asks what it is you would like to do and what it is you're good at as opposed to what you've fallen into,' says Neil Carr, human resources director of the Group Purchasing Division of SmithKline Beecham (SB).

Back in 1992/3 Carr decided that something more needed to be done to tackle the issue from a corporate viewpoint. He was then European personnel director of SB's animal health division (which has since been sold to Pfizer). He was taking an MBA at Kingston Business School and chose as his thesis what companies should do to help managers plan their careers at a time when job security was fast disappearing and delayering was playing havoc with traditional forms of career progression. As it happened, the animal health division was itself undergoing restructuring, which involved some delayering.

So Carr put together a questionnaire to find out how SB managers were reacting to the radical changes taking place in the corporate environment. They were asked how they perceived the changes, how their authority was affected and what were their career expectations in the light of the changed circumstances. They were also asked what they felt their power base was in the company and how that had been affected and how that impacted on their attitudes to the company in general. What was not possible now that had been possible before the changes?

This exercise was followed up by a career development workshop supervised by independent consultants who assessed a group of SB managers against a set of competencies which had been identified as those that were most likely to prevail in the company in future. Neil Carr recalls: 'My problem statement in my MBA thesis was that delayering has an adverse affect on careers, but really what I was trying to do was test out that assumption in terms of how people actually perceived that kind of change. How do they actually see their career in terms of their prospects when this kind of delayering and restructuring occurs? What they felt the organization should do. What they were going to do about it if the organization didn't do something.'

Carr also investigated what other companies were doing to come up with creative solutions to the problem. It came as no great surprise to him that very little was being done by any company. The SB survey did, however, throw up some fascinating findings. He says: 'Interestingly enough, they actually felt that their work output and their interest in the work had increased since the changes and they quite enjoyed the new work environment. However, their perception of what the company was doing in terms of career progression was very negative. I had made a conscious effort to put in place a lot of training and development opportunities, but they didn't see any opportunities for career progression. They certainly didn't see any structured way of progressing to the next level.'

The first thought of the surveyed managers was that their options had shrunk dramatically as a result of the delayering. They could not see where they were going to progress to. Secondly, they did not feel anyone in the company was sitting down with them to address the problem in a structured way.

Carr admits that SB, like most companies, had abdicated this responsibility, arguing that what the new work environment called for was self-development. This, in his view, is not the way to solve the problem:

'The good people will develop themselves for sure, but they develop in a direction that is not necessarily in line with the rest of the organization and what we started to see was the good people leaving. Good people will always find jobs because they're always in short supply. They've been developing themselves in the direction that suits them and something comes up on the network and they're off.'

Inevitably the concept of employability crept into SB's considered approach to deal with the problem: 'It's not about career progression or loyalty to the employee anymore; it's about employability, about us making you so marketable that if there are no more opportunities in SB someone else will come and take you. That's fine if the company actually does something positive about that – if you proactively go out and create an environment where people can self-develop because they have access to development materials on an open or distance learning basis or if they have access to workshops or you have a programme where you rotate people. It's fine if you multi-skill them by moving them into different functions, you allow them to work on projects and you empower them to make decisions by giving them projects where they are accountable. If you positively manage that in the organization – it is just the tip of the iceberg – but you start to address the problem.'

Even that, however, is a distant ideal for most companies, according to Carr's research: 'Companies talk a lot about multi-skilling but in reality it's very difficult to do. If, for example, you want to take someone out of marketing and stick them into research, the disciplines are so fundamentally different. You have to ask if there is a business case for doing it. Even if you assume there is, many companies will say it won't work because the disciplines are so different. They don't take the time to try to make it work. It requires effort and resolve to do it.'

One of the problems Carr has identified is the fact that in today's highly competitive environment every person in an organization is expected to add value from the first day of arrival in a new department. Nobody is given the time to learn. Carr's solution would be to add a development slot to every department's head count. In an organization of twenty people, for example, there ought to be one extra slot funded by head office that is specifically there for development: 'That person would do a normal job in the department, but there would be a planned and co-ordinated structure that would allow people to develop. It would also be easier to rotate people because you would have a structure to do it. It is very difficult to do job rotation if you don't have any flexibility. Somebody has got to move before somebody else can move into the slot. It has to snowball. If there's no vacancy to move into and you can't create a slot, it's very difficult to do.'

Simply providing the funding to let employees do their own development is abdicating a company's responsibility, in Carr's view. Nor does he consider it practical from the company's point of view. It will result in good people leaving the organization, which might be acceptable in terms of sales and marketing functions, for example, but causes serious continuity problems in knowledge-based industries. R&D is a good example. As Neil Carr points out: 'Good science doesn't just happen overnight. It takes years to develop. I have certainly explored the possibility of looking at jobs and putting a three-year maximum ceiling on them and taking people on for a three-year contract and then letting them go. But you're looking at a very few functions where continuity is not an issue. It might work with general management skills – transferable skills – but in the pharmaceutical industry you need people who know a lot about that industry. Certainly, organizations like SB will have to look more at doing that, but at the moment it is still very traditional.'

Carr is using the findings from his career aspirations survey to work out some basic principles and concepts for future application in SB. 'The main finding was that we have to take a much more proactive approach to this and we have to start creating an environment where individuals can develop themselves but where we give them access to the tools and methods to develop and stretch them.'

That will mean formalizing job rotation and project management, which SB is already beginning to do. It also means formalizing succession planning where people in SB are moved through different divisions or through different sectors and their progress is tracked. Carr estimates it will be a good five years before such programmes start to show encouraging results.

However, Carr argues that an even more fundamental approach is called for, starting at school: 'You need to get to people before they leave school. Currently, there is no career advice in terms of managing a career at school. You are simply asked what job you want to do. Do you want to be a doctor or a lawyer or do you want to go into the police or the armed forces? That kind of thing. Maybe, if you're lucky, a couple of local companies will come in and ask if you would like to join them.'

Until the issue is tackled as part of basic education, there is unlikely to be any change in traditional attitudes about career progression. 'If someone told me that I was not going to go any higher up the corporate ladder, that I was going to stay where I am now, I wouldn't be happy with that at all. I am still part of the generation where success is about going up the ladder. This is a fundamental building block. Unless you change that attitude, people of my generation are never going to be happy with standing still.

'The current solution to the corporate ladder problem is moving people down and completely changing what they are doing. The analogy I use is from marketing to chemistry. It's a fundamental change so you feel you're starting again. You go through a kind of renewal.'

Carr believes that as major corporations pursue closer partnerships with, for example, their suppliers, opportunities will increasingly arise to move people around more imaginatively. There will be less constraint on finding appropriate slots to move people into for development purposes. It could also help to reduce the stigma attached to moving people into jobs that seem to be a demotion or at best a lateral move. 'As networking or partnerships become more of a reality, particularly supplier relationships, you have opportunities to move people into the supply function and vice versa. It's a kind of glorified job rotation, but each time you do that you could actually be moving to a higher level. It's only by doing that you achieve real partnership, if you think about it.'

Job titles would become obsolete in a world in which people are rotated around an organization to gain broader experience and make them more employable. The job ceases to be about where a person is in the hierarchy. It then revolves around what the business needs and what the person produces.

Career development workshops

To help managers in the animal health division gain a more realistic idea of career expectations, Neil Carr invited an outside consultancy that specializes in career management to run a three-day workshop. The managers were assessed against the core competencies that had been identified as necessary for the division's future success. Carr recalls: 'We looked at where the organization was going, what were the core competencies the organization required for its future development. They included things like team-working and innovation – fairly generic competencies, but crucial for SB.'

Managers from all levels in the organization were observed during the workshop by specially trained assessors to ascertain to what extent their behaviour demonstrated skills in the identified competencies. They were not told what the competencies were until the end of the programme to avoid them adapting their natural behaviour in favour of what they thought would match the competencies. Some standard psychometric tests were used to identify personality traits.

John O'Brien was the career adviser SB called in to supervise the workshop. He recalls: 'What we were trying to do was say: here's where the business is going, layers have been taken out and it is important that you take stock of where you are in terms of your career, where there are areas for personal growth and so forth. But let's face it, it's dead men's shoes and there aren't many of them going to die.

'There were various inputs in terms of career structure and how careers plateau and where the power base is. OK, you have a PhD in microbiology or whatever it is – is that your power base? In which case do you want to change? Are you within your comfort zone? We used a mixture of exercises, inputs and psychometrics with personal counselling. The whole output of that was a very short report back to the company.

'It wasn't an assessment centre in the full sense of the word. There was a short report, which the individual got a copy of, to his or her boss for a discussion within two weeks of the workshop ending. But the main idea was a learning experience for people to take stock of where they'd got to, where they wanted to go, what factors they wanted to consider. Did they want to be promoted? Did they want to go higher? Did they want to move sideways? The aim was to give them enough information geared against the competencies required by the business – it was very focused on the business as well – to see how it stacked up.'

Says Carr: 'We actually had people afterwards saying that it was the first time they had experienced what management was really about within SB and that it was the first time they had had the opportunity to demonstrate their levels of skill in some of the management competencies.'

It was enough for some of them to decide that they did not want to make a career in management. It convinced them that they were happy to stay as a back room chemist or a sales person. Others found that their interest in management was heightened.

Carr accepted from the start that it was a risky exercise and that some of those taking part might reach the conclusion that there was a mismatch between their identified skills and the core competencies that were needed to take SB into the future. He says: 'What I wanted was a position where people actually set some very clear expectations about where they were really going to go from a career point of view and whether they should really be thinking about management at this stage. What we didn't say was: you'll never become a manager, because people will change. What we were saying was, at this stage, given the competencies required of a manager within SB, this is the gap. This is where you need to be to get to the first level and you're really here. You can see the task. Now it's your decision how you want to take that forward. We didn't lose anybody, but I am sure there will be people who will change their career as a result of it and I accept that they may go and join another company. Or they may decide to stay where they are; they don't want to go into management. They might change the job they are doing, but at the same level. We've also had people who have started to develop their skills in a more structured way, because the idea was that they would go back and discuss the findings of the workshop with their line manager.'

What kind of support should companies be giving to employees who want to take more charge of their own careers? Carr believes:

'It can be anything from providing a resource centre and having trained counsellors on board who people can actually go to and say: Here is my development plan. What's the best way of tackling this?

And do some analysis in terms of the learning preferences or the learning style, fit the appropriate methods to you. Do you want to do distance learning or open learning? Is it better for you to have a formal course arrangement? What on-job training can you do? What combination of on-job and off-job etc.? You can do anything from that kind of resource and giving people access to that in the most sophisticated ways, to doing nothing more than: there's the plan, go away and give me some ideas on how you're going to tackle it.'

How does Neil Carr see SB improving the opportunities for self-development and career development in the future?

'I hope we start to look in more detail at some of the ways to formalize an approach where we can actually access talent, where we can get people on development programmes and actually do something about them. We are beginning to do that. We are making progress and we've put some good processes in place. I hope we start to take more responsibility for creating an environment where people can develop themselves and, more importantly, we can develop them by giving them a lot of on-job opportunities, because on-job opportunities can be much more powerful when you get into management areas than more formal courses.

'There's no doubt that for most people experiential learning stays longer in the mind. If we can start doing that in terms of multi-skilling, job rotation, project management, empowerment – formalizing that – creating an environment where that really is part of the culture . . . but we really are at the early days with that and it is going to be four to five years before a company of this size can achieve that.'

CASE STUDY: Sun Life Assurance Society

Another company that has used core competencies to align corporate goals with individual career progression is Sun Life Assurance Society, which has undergone a major restructuring and culture change in the past five years. This has included moving from an organization structure with six or seven levels to one with only two layers of management. As part of that change process, there is now a focus on skills and competencies that has enabled it to replace an out-moded grading structure where people could only be promoted into a new job if there was a vacancy. Under the new approach, achievement of a combination of measurable outputs, competencies and skills provides movement through a very wide pay range. This has completely removed the need for job evaluation across these roles. For case managers to move through this pay range, the company has closely defined sets of trigger points which combine the three critical factors of measurable outputs, competencies and skills.

The case manager role has been developed on the basis of the role as a career in its own right. As such, competencies in particular play an increasingly important role in the case manager's progression through the trigger points. The company has clearly defined the behaviours required at each trigger point on the pay range.

For those managers who want to progress in other roles within the organization, competency models exist for all broad levels in Sun Life. This provides a focus for development for individuals wishing to pursue alternative roles, such as team leader or training officer.

Sun Life believes that the benefits of applying competencies to career progression are manifold:

- Individuals know what is expected of them both within current roles and for future progression. There is a clear focus on what is required for individuals to perform their jobs and for case managers in particular there is a clear path of progression with competencies through trigger points.
- There is a clear message within the organization that doing your job is not enough. Individuals need to be seen to add value by broadening their experience and taking on additional responsibilities, such as project work.
- Competencies are defined for each role and each level within the organization. Therefore individuals can develop their career map by reference to the requirements of each role.
- Clearly defined competencies and accountabilities for each role in the organization enable individuals to plan their personal development to achieve their career aims. The level of personal ownership for career development is heightened with individuals having more control over their destiny and a greater say in their development.
- Through the performance management system, an individual's behavioural performance is objectively measured and feedback is given through the appraisal process. This increased personal awareness of performance leads to a greater understanding of

125

personal strengths and weaknesses, and a clearer focus for personal development.

- There is an emphasis on soft skills *and* hard skills in the organization. This is a cultural shift away from regarding a job as process-oriented and hard skill focused to a broader, more holistic view of roles within Sun Life, combining both the technical and behavioural aspects of a role.

The central training function of Sun Life has reassessed the core training programmes to take account of the desired behaviours. In addition, a lot of groundwork has been carried out to position competencies and enhance peoples' understanding of them prior to using them as part of the performance management process. There is now an explicit link between the company's core training programmes and its core competencies.

At the same time, the company is encouraging greater emphasis on self-development and has invested in an open learning centre to provide further opportunities for individuals to improve their skills and broaden their knowledge.

The company has identified through staff consultation exercises that career progression issues within a flatter organization are a keen concern of its staff. It has established a project group to look into the issues, with two broad objectives:

- to consider how the company can understand individuals' career aspirations and give them more help/information to plan their careers
- to illustrate different career paths open to individuals.

The company's first step has been to introduce an annual career development discussion. The aims of this discussion are: to give each individual the opportunity to discuss career aspirations; to assess their competency strengths and weaknesses in relation to their aspirations; to gain a better understanding of themselves.

Sun Life Assurance has produced a booklet entitled *Managing Our Futures* which outlines the processes within the organization that support career management. The approach has been to ask line staff to develop these processes to encourage ownership of them, and to ensure their practicality in the customer service environment.

The company also undertakes regular reviews of its competency models to ensure they continue to reflect both the strategic direction of the organization and the roles within Sun Life. This is a joint process between line staff and personnel staff. From the broad competency output, the company encourages customization of behavioural examples within locations to reflect more accurately the behaviours required in particular roles, in particular areas of the organization.

CASE STUDY: The Post Office

The Post Office has been undergoing the most profound changes in its 350-year history. These changes, both externally imposed and internally driven, have had asignificant impact on career patterns within the organization. Organizational restructuring has involved:

- Large reduction in the size of HQ operations
- Much greater decentralization to geographically devolved units
- Downsizing and the use of assessment centres on a substantial scale for making appointments to the new structures.

It is believed that the assessment centres for the Royal Mail, which involved 12,000 people in total, is the largest exercise of its kind ever carried out in the UK. The result of all this, according to Gwen Wileman, strategic training manager, The Post Office Training and Development Group, is: 'We now have a flatter, more rapidly responsive and more customer-focused organization. Inevitably there are a number of disbenefits of such restructuring. Flat structures themselves challenge the traditional concept of management at all levels. We have to learn again and train again to ensure the new organization works. Restructuring has also altered the age profile of our business quite dramatically and a career for life is less and less likely.'

At the group level The Post Office has introduced an approach to career development, which according to Wileman, is 'not in the old prescriptive way, but as a partnership between individual and organisation'. She sees this as the key to developing the organization's existing managerial talent: 'The use of business education as a means of working on live issues affecting the corporation as a whole, is crucial to our organizational learning.

'Although there is still a long way to go, the intention is to further the concept of "willingness to learn" at all levels of the business. We have begun to build an integrated portfolio of business and management education/training programmes matched to business objectives and linked to career development for individuals.'

There are four levels of business education programmes designed to ensure the organization's management population moves through significant internal learning events at critical times in their careers. Insists Wileman: 'In a flatter organization we must ensure important learning is not left to chance.'

Additionally, managers are recommended and selected for external business school programmes. The Post Office regards it as vital to position the external programmes within its own strategic framework, so that it can be sure they add value at the right time in a person's career and at the right time for its business development plans.

In the context of most effectively ensuring management continuity, The Post Office is currently reviewing its succession and career planning system with the aim of helping individuals to develop their own careers along paths that connect and interconnect with the formal components of its management education and development framework. Gwen Wileman adds: 'We are designing development workshops to assist the business and individuals with competency gap and training and development reviews. These processes emphasize both the self-assessment and self-development aspects of individuals' future learning needs and the importance of matching individual development programmes with the requirements of the business.'

The workshops comprise two linked events. At the first event participants are introduced to a model which will help them in building their plans, and asked to decide on the parts of the model which are of greatest importance to them. After an interval of four to six weeks, they return to take part in the development workshop itself in which they finalize their plans and 'test' them with the help of other participants. Line managers are invited to attend the first day of the workshop and to agree the final plans.

Royal Mail

Royal Mail – one of The Post Office's four trading companies – is introducing structured management development processes as part of the group-wide effort. This includes the introduction of a systematic approach to measurement of an individual's performance and his or her development and training needs, which is based on competencies, and secondly, the use of independent assessment processes to complement individual line managers' assessments.

In 1992, the management structure of Royal Mail was reduced from nine to five levels below the managing director and some 3,000 people left the business, the majority at middle manager level. Wileman notes: 'The age distribution of Royal Mail's current managers shows a somewhat skewed profile with few managers in their fifties and a younger average age than ever before. The flatter structure has itself reduced opportunities for promotion. The combination of a younger management profile, recession, and a more stable organizational environment means relative stagnation in opportunities for movement. The business recognizes the need to stimulate development.'

As a consequence, Royal Mail has introduced a management development policy designed to re-equip and invigorate existing managers and prepare them and others for future roles in the business. The key features are:

- to maximize individual potential – not necessarily focused on promotability
- to ensure high-quality resource at all managerial levels, preferably through the development of its own people
- all employees to have appropriate development and training opportunities
- to provide a pool of successors for all jobs.

The Royal Mail learning strategy identifies competence analysis as the foundation to informed recruitment, selection, performance assessment and training and development activity. Work was recently completed on the development of key managerial capabilities to ensure that these reflect business needs. Job competency profiles are being published so that all employees are aware of them and can have a clear indication of directions needed in their development if they aspire to progress through the organization to more senior roles.

A number of career development initiatives have been introduced by Royal Mail:

- *Directions*. This is a national initiative for post men and women.

It is jointly funded by Royal Mail and the Department of Employment and provides opportunities for individuals to plan their careers.

- *Career Horizons.* Following the 1992 restructuring, research was carried out at Royal Mail into the morale of plateaued managers – the effect on their loyalty to the organization, motivation and overall performance compared to non-plateaued managers. In addition, evidence was gathered about what would help in terms of organizational effort to assist their career development. From this research base a programme of career development workshops emerged called Career Horizons.
- *Senior management resourcing.* A process to identify employees who have the ability and potential for senior management appointments was introduced in 1995 at Royal Mail in Scotland and Northern Ireland. First line and non-managerial grades were eligible and prospective candidates needed to demonstrate commitment to undertake development activity – in their own time.

The Post Office is attempting to manage proactively the effects of changing career patterns at all levels. The key strands of its approach are:

- The use of research to ensure development strategies are business-focused and support individuals' needs.
- An integrated business education and career planning process which is crucial to The Post Office-wide development activities.
- A competency-based approach to assessment and development.
- Career development right across the organization is seen as a partnership between the individual and the business.
- The line manager as coach is key. This concept has been enthusiastically supported by some of the most senior people within The Post Office.
- 'Learning for all' is essential if The Post Office is to maximize the potential of all its employees.

Gwen Wileman sums up: 'We are seeking to encourage our employees to be innovative and empower them to learn. For individuals to succeed we are creating opportunities to develop skills and abilities to enhance their competencies and employability. We are expecting individuals to take responsibility for their own career development as traditional ladders disappear and we are supporting this in many ways.

'For business success we are ensuring the integration of management development and career development, increasing the involvement of business leaders in training and development with learning focused on achieving business objectives.'

What unites these three case studies are:

- the proactive approach of the organizations involved
- their use of competencies to provide a formal framework of development and to replace 'experience blocks' as promotion qualifiers
- their insistence that career development is a joint activity
- their response to the problems created by downsizing and delayering.

These organizations have begun to address the fears that delayering brings and to create opportunities for those who want to seize them. They are revising their reward systems to move away from the idea that only by being promoted could a manager boost her earnings. In the SmithKline Beecham case there is even an explicit recognition that the result of the development may be that people decide to move to another organization. By making explicit their competency frameworks, the organizations are providing individuals with clear guidance as to the benefits and costs of development or non-development.

Yet some questions remain. Do the competency frameworks adopted reflect current performance requirements or do they anticipate the future? If they anticipate the future, how accurate are they? In a more rapidly changing world it is also more difficult to forecast competency requirements. How long does it take to develop the required competencies? What are the implications for the length of the learning period for the organization's flexibility? In so far as the competency framework is the foundation for the new structures of career management or career planning, what determines whether this is seen as an instrument of organizational control, with its rigid prescriptions of appropriate behaviour, or as a helpful framework for individual development? The new processes place a lot of responsibility and demands on line managers. How well are line managers coping with these demands and responsibilities in the context of delayered organizations?

Chapter Eight

The Tools and Framework for Career Planning

Most of the UK companies that are attempting to develop their career management programmes and match organizational needs with individual career ambitions would admit that they are still at the formative stage and that there is a considerable amount of pioneering work to be done. In the United States, however, career management has reached a higher level of sophistication, particularly in the Silicon Valley in California, where innovation is a way of life. There, such companies as Sun Microsystems, Rachem and Apple have set up career management centres, which the *Harvard Business Review* describes as 'havens where employees can go to work on self-assessment, receive counselling, and attend seminars on, say, how to conduct an effective job interview or how to network'.

Robert H. Waterman Jr, Judith A. Waterman and Betsy A. Collard, the authors of the article on the career-resilient workforce, argue that the establishment of a career management centre helps a programme to gain credibility: 'They are places where employees can obtain career reference materials, check on internal and external job openings, contribute to discussions on business strategy, and, most important, learn how to think strategically about their own careers.'

The *Harvard Business Review* article stresses that the location of such centres is very important: 'By making it highly visible and easily accessible, the company sends the message that it is not only acceptable but desirable for employees to use it. The opposite message may be sent by locating it off the beaten track.'

Cable & Wireless in the UK has set up a Career Action Centre in London to provide a focus for career management. The original impetus was the need to equip expatriate managers with information to manage their international careers, but demand has been so great that the company has since set up a centre in Ireland and plans further facilities in the Caribbean and Hong Kong. The centres provide help with assessment, career planning and development. Sue Tomlinson, C&W director of international resourcing and development, told *Management Today* for an article that appeared in the November 1995 issue: 'This is very much within the focus of business needs, particularly motivating and retaining good people.' She recognizes that the counterpart to developing people's marketability and sense of their own worth is giving them the opportunity to use it. Informing people of vacancies and upcoming projects within the business units is a key part of the centres' function. The centres are self-funding and they would not have been developed at such speed if demand or willingness to pay had been lacking.

At each of its major sites Rover Group has established a learning centre with access to computer-based training, books, interactive video and courses on a range of subjects. To encourage learning, the Rover Employee Assisted Learning Scheme offers £100 towards an external training programme on a topic not related directly to an employee's job. To help employees, known as associates, reassess themselves, their aspirations and their careers, Rover has more recently opened the Resourcing Centre at Longbridge. It offers informal and completely confidential discussions on individuals' job situations and the options open to them. All internal vacancies are advertised, as well as vacancies with other organizations, especially suppliers, plus information about re-training, financial planning and small business start up.

CASE STUDY: Sun Microsystems

California-based Sun Microsystems has a strong reputation for having developed a career management service for its employees that has established some firm ground rules. The US company boasts a career centre and a career management services (CMS) department for its employees that is well in advance of what many companies aspire to.

134

A CMS team has been established to help employees make informed and creative career decisions. The company regards career management as a partnership between employees and management and claims that it provides 'the tools, resources, training and information' its employees and work teams need in order to 'thrive in these changing times'. These aim to help employees:

- learn more about employment trends and job enrichment at Sun
- create or update an individual's career road map
- access expert help to make important career decisions
- revitalize or create a new work team
- explore new opportunities at Sun *or elsewhere*.

A core value at Sun Microsystems is: 'We acknowledge the essential link between company growth and development of individuals.' The concept acknowledges:

- rapid changes in business environments require continuous learning for all employees
- Sun Microsystems' future success depends on employees with leading-edge skills
- career management is a partnership between employees and management
- enabling employees to be 'career flexible' and self-reliant is a competitive advantage in today's global market-place.

The California company regards career self-reliance as an important skill for employability, which it defines as: 'The ability to actively manage your work life in a rapidly changing environment and the attitude of being self-employed whether you are inside or outside the organization.'

CMS supports employees in a variety of ways. The back-up comes in two main areas:

- *Proactive*: Personalized services and programmes designed and delivered by professional career counsellors. They help individuals or work teams to solve unique career challenges, seek new opportunities with Sun Microsystems and develop and take action on long-term career plans.

135

- *Transition*: If work is reduced or outsourced CMS can deliver transition plans customized to suit the schedules and business needs of individuals and groups. Referrals to external outplacement agencies are available.

Sun Microsystems acknowledges that managing a career means different things to different people, but the company assures it employees: 'No matter what motivates your career inquiry, we offer a comprehensive, integrated solution. This approach enables you or your work group to gain knowledge, either one step at a time or in an accelerated, intense form.'

Among the services on offer at Sun Microsystems are the following:

- *Career Talk*: Career experts lead dialogues on career trends, techniques and skills.

- *Seminars and Workshops* are held on career success topics. These include:
    Career self-reliance
    What is career success?
    Career growth
    Introduction to the company's career library
    Updating your résumé
    Interactive interviewing skills
    Networking

- *One-to-One Career Counselling*: Each employee is eligible for two hours of complementary career counselling each year. Honest and confidential guidance is provided by professional counsellors.

- *A Career Library* is equipped with a comprehensive collection of business books on career management techniques, occupations, trends and industries. It also contains a range of video and audio tapes featuring expert opinions on hot career topics. A library specialist helps target an individual's research.

- *Career Centre Tours* are arranged for individuals or teams. Free day passes are provided to visit the Career Action Center at Palo Alto (see pages 107–9).

- *Career Speakers* are provided to stimulate career management dialogues at staff meetings or off-site.

- *Career Transition Services*: Customized services to suit specific needs of groups or individuals. The services include seminars, workshops, professional career counselling and administrative staff.

- *Job Listings*: Internal postings from Sun Microsystems plus over 5,000 current listings from companies in northern California.

- *Tips*: Weekly peer brainstorming groups

Proof of the pudding
Sun Microsystems advises its employees that career self-assessment lays the foundation for enhanced career management by helping people to benchmark and appreciate what they are today, their current strengths, preferred work environment and the way they work best. It points out that research has shown that people whose work is highly aligned with their skills, interests, values and style experienced increased career satisfaction. Career satisfaction is, in turn, related to increased motivation and productivity on the job.

In the April 1995 issue of *The Career Network*, the company outlines success stories featuring people who have made use of its career self-assessment techniques and services:

- *A burned-out sales manager* sought counselling at Sun Micro-systems' Career Center. Sorting skill cards helped him understand that he was using detail and analytical skills he no longer enjoyed. Rating himself high in relationship and communication skills, he found an account manager position at Sun Microsystems where he could work directly with customers.

- *A design engineer* with a doctorate seemingly had it all, but something was missing. Working with assessment instruments and a Sun Microsystems career counsellor, he understood that providing quality service and connecting with customers were essential for his career satisfaction. He decided to explore a career shift into Sun Microsystems' technical marketing or systems engineering groups.

- *A project co-ordinator*, fearing a reorganization, complained she could not look for a job because she had no skills. After working with 'Skillscan' cards, which identify a person's favoured abilities, she clearly saw the skills she had and wrote a résumé presenting these strengths.

- *An engineer,* who felt unsure after becoming a manager, was able to pinpoint the new skills he needed by using the 'Career Architect' assessment technique which identifies key interpersonal and organizational skills.

- *A technical writer* with two young children gained the courage to negotiate with her manager to telecommute part of her work week after clarifying her values using the Edgar Schein 'Career Anchor' technique (see Chapter Five). She identified 'lifestyle' as a major career anchor.

- *A finance manager,* who was stressed at work, rated high in adventure on the 'Strong Interest Inventory', which analyses personal interests. The computer-scored profile compares a person's pattern of occupation likes/dislikes to groups of satisfied people in 200 occupations. It helped the finance manager realize that he needed to balance work with his favourite leisure-time activity of horseback riding.

- *A software developer* wanted new challenges and career growth, but did not think she would like to manage people. The 'Myers-Briggs Type Indicator' (MBTI) confirmed that managers with her style tend to be impatient with long-term people management, but have excellent project management abilities she could use in her career. MBTI helps managers understand their style for relating to people, gathering information, making decisions and organizing work.

- *A document manager* who attended a 'Career Design Workshop', realized she wanted to do more analytical work. She shared this information with her manager who restructured the job to include more of her analytical skills and interests.

CASE STUDY: Hoskyns Group

Hoskyns, the UK arm of Cap Gemini Sogeti, the leading European IT services company, does not have a career centre as such. Instead, it has a detailed framework for supporting its managers and staff in their personal career ambitions. The company has drawn up career maps for all its main job roles, which itemize the skills, experience and attributes needed. Each employee is encouraged to keep a career portfolio and there are detailed guidelines on how to progress in many of the key jobs in the company. Staff within the organization can work on many different assignments throughout the year, and therefore, could have many different managers. To ensure continuity, each individual has a staff manager he or she can turn to for advice on career moves and progression.

The essence of the work carried out by Hoskyns ranges from advice and guidance, system building and development, education and training, right through to the total management of complex IT systems for its clients. Project management is a key activity of the group and project managers are the superstars of its workforce and much sought after. Because of the nature of its work, Hoskyns is a very fluid organization that demands great flexibility on the part of its staff. Carolyn Nimmy, a divisional director responsible for human resource management, sums it up: 'The challenge for us is to manage a diverse workforce of highly flexible, highly mobile, very bright, intelligent and demanding individuals, combined with very solid performers focused on service-oriented work, who are happy not to be challenged quite so much. You don't want a company full of superstars.'

Adding to the complexity of Hoskyns' organization mix is the fact that it sometimes takes over complete responsibility for the human resource management of whole departments that have been outsourced by its clients, including the salary and benefits packages. So the former employees of client organizations can suddenly find themselves a part of a dynamic, flexible group, where career mobility and constant upgrading of skills is an integral part of the culture. For some this can open up exciting new career prospects; for others the culture shock involved is far from welcome.

In keeping with such a fluid structure, Hoskyns is constantly reviewing its own organizational needs. For the past two years it has been undertaking a major revamp of its career management and development policies, partly as a result of a major restructuring exercise. Explains Nimmy:

'As a management services company what we sell basically is our people. We don't manufacture hardware, so people are our fee revenue earner. With the more traditional hierarchical structure of the company we found that we were creating good business managers but somewhere along the line we were not doing enough to promote some of the business-related roles like service management. At the same time, like many companies, we started to flatten out and go through a change in the hierarchical structure. This meant we needed to develop multi-capability managers of the business who would be managing and be responsible for their part of the management structure and then have very senior individuals who might be a project director handling a £25 million to £50 million project. For example, one of our senior directors was actually managing the major contract we recently undertook for British Gas.'

Hoskyns realized that as its organization flattened out and there were far greater opportunities for its people to move around, it needed to provide a lot more information about the roles within the organization and the opportunities that existed for career development. It also felt the need to encourage people to be thinking continually about their market worth, not because it wanted to encourage people to leave, but because the more marketable they became the more they could earn and do a better job for the company. The company wanted to move towards striking a mutually-beneficial partnership with its staff and away from the old-style parent-child relationship. This also meant trying to persuade staff to take greater responsibility for managing their own careers, but within a framework of guidance and opportunities provided by the group.

To underline the importance it attaches to career management and development, Hoskyns has introduced the idea that every individual must have a staff manager who is specifically responsible for this area. It means that some people can have three managers responsible for their progression in the company. They can have a *project manager* who is responsible for an individual's daily tasks and motivation and who conducts regular assignment reviews. They can also have a *business unit manager*, the person who has organizational responsibility for an individual and who decides on that person's salary and benefits. If the business manager is supervising perhaps 200 or 300 people he or she will hardly be in a position to know everyone individually, particularly as people are being constantly moved around. Therefore, Hoskyns has introduced the concept of a *staff manager* who is responsible for bringing together input from all the different assignments an individual undertakes and probably from the business manager as well. The staff manager carries out performance reviews and discusses with an individual his or her career management and development on a one-to-one basis.

Carolyn Nimmy shies away from using the word mentor, because the staff manager has a formal responsibility to carry out a performance review as well as being available to give career advice and guidance. She adds: 'One of the reasons for providing so much information about career opportunities is to assist the staff manager, because if you are in a project group you might understand what is happening in projects, but you might not understand what opportunities exist at a good data centre down the road. With this information to hand, the staff manager can sit down with an individual and discuss his or her strengths and weaknesses and core competencies and the kind of development and experience needed to make a career move.'

The approach Hoskyns has adopted is highly flexible. Says Nimmy: 'In some instances you could be an operator in a data centre and your assignment manager and business manager and staff manager might all be the same person. We have to have flexibility in the way we manage people to recognize the different types of services we provide to our customers. So we have tried with career management to give individuals information and to encourage them so that they can see the opportunities across the group. They can then think about the sort of role they want to take on. They then realize that they don't need to have a large number of people reporting to them in order to progress. They can become the best technical architect in the company and get to director level because of their technical capability and skill. As they get to more senior levels in the company they need to have interpersonal skills as well. These can't be ignored.'

This recognition of technical ability is reflected in the salary scales of Hoskyns. A technically-oriented senior manager or a project director can be among the top one per cent earners in the company. The company is at pains to avoid the old-style approach that technically skilled people can only progress up the hierarchy if they become general managers. Highly skilled technical people in Hoskyns are held in great esteem and their pay packets reflect that regard. Project managers can win or lose significant contracts for the company. They are pivotal to its success and this is underscored by the rewards they receive.

At the same time, Hoskyns recognizes that it is competing in the market-place for a scarce resource. As Britain comes out of the worst recession for many years, the IT market has exploded. Hoskyns is recruiting, according to Nimmy, 'like there's no tomorrow. We can't get enough good people. Turnover in the IT industry at the moment is a problem because there are only a few good people and everybody is poaching other companies' people. So the high-flyers are moving from company to company to achieve a nice hike in their earnings. We have become a bit self-destructive because we are putting inflationary pressures on our own salaries because everybody is after the same sort of people.'

Unlike many companies, Hoskyns continued to recruit graduates during the recession and there is now great danger that other organizations, trying to catch up, will try to poach these graduates who now have two years' experience behind them. However, Hoskyns believes it has the edge over banks and small IT departments in other companies in that it can offer flexibility of opportunity and the chance to have a very varied career within one operation. In a group of 4,300 people there are a host of different roles – the company has identified something like 100 throughout the organization. Within those there are certain key roles that have been defined in greater detail because of their importance to the success of the business. For example, a lot of work has gone into defining the core competencies for the project manager role, because it can be a very high-risk job and one that is crucial to the group's survival. Assessment centres are used to recruit and promote people into such pivotal roles.

The wide variety of jobs available provides individuals working for Hoskyns with the opportunity to move around the organization freely and easily. Says Nimmy: 'Part of the culture of the organization is that you can get on and do things. We are not highly bureaucratic in the respect that you can't move without getting forms signed in triplicate. We try to provide support, frameworks and guidelines, so we can retain our entrepreneurial spirit. People like the work environment to be that way. We have a good reputation in the market-place. Even though we may not always pay the top rates, we are seen as a very good employer.'

Internal job vacancies are posted both electronically and on notice boards and through house publications. Business units have a resource allocator who, with the aid of a skills database, provides information about available staff when a particular job needs filling. They try to match assignments against the people in a particular business unit. People anxious to gain experience of a new type of project work can contact both their staff manager and the resource allocator in their department to let it be known they are keen to make a move. They can specify the kind of assignments they are looking for to help with their own career development needs. It is not always possible to achieve a perfect fit, but Hoskyns has put in place the system that ensures every effort is made to satisfy career-ambitious individuals.

Meritocracy?

Documentation setting out Hoskyns' career management and development policies is available to everyone in the company. It explains with great clarity the philosophy behind the group's policies and gives advice on how to manage a career. There are practical details about what is available in the company's human resource library. It emphasizes that Hoskyns operates along the lines of a meritocracy. As Carolyn Nimmy says: 'Meritocracy is a difficult word to use but that is what we say we are – you get somewhere because of your personal performance. In the US that is sometimes seen as being against team-work. We say team-work is very important, so we try not to be too purist about the word meritocracy. We are saying you don't get on by years of service; you get on by your own personal performance and your market worth. You will get rewarded accordingly.'

To help achieve a match between the business needs of Hoskyns and the career aspirations of its managers, the group has developed career maps which list all the key roles in the company and where they are likely to occur and how far up the organization they are likely to take a person. A programmer analyst, for example, will see at a glance that he or she has no chance of becoming a director without moving into new roles – but a team leader in applications management, for example, can see from the guidelines that there is an opportunity to become a team leader in project management if there is a desire to expand his or her career experience. There is a career map for each core part of the business in each of Hoskyns' service lines. Somebody in applications management, for example, can study the career maps to find out if there are any potential opportunities in software development or in projects or something of that nature.

The career maps also provide information about the knowledge, skills and experience needed at the entry level of a key role. These are the essential qualifications for the job. Some of the requirements are mandatory; others are merely desirable. People wanting to become a systems analyst, for example, will learn that they need to hone their time management and report writing skills. In terms of experience, they are obviously expected to be IT aware, to have done some

143

programming and to have dealt with users. On the knowledge side, an understanding of systems design is desirable. The 'must have' qualifications are printed in capitals. Adds Nimmy: 'We make exceptions but it really focuses people's ideas. If you want to become a systems analyst, for example, and you are programming at the moment, you should realize that you need to go on a report writing course and to be given an opportunity on a project to write a report on something you have done and to do some problem analysis. You could apply time management to how you manage those two aspects.'

Key responsibilities are listed under each of the job roles. These include such attributes as the ability to communicate and analyse. In addition, the development programme, outlining the different courses it would be beneficial to attend, is listed under each key role. Once you have moved into the new job, what are the training programmes that would help you advance? The depth of the information, which is available both electronically and on paper, is in direct proportion to the seniority of the job. Project management is a key role at the top end of the scale. Therefore, the skills and experience requirements, as well as the development programme, are given far greater coverage.

The career map is meant to be read at a glance, but it is supported by something Hoskyns calls a 'role blueprint', which is a more detailed breakdown of the key roles. It also contains information about experience indicators and things of that nature.

Hoskyns arrived at the criteria to define each job role through a series of workshops conducted across the organization. It started at the top of the company with a workshop of twenty people from a service line who brainstormed the skills, experience and competencies that each job required. The definitions this group came up with were then cascaded down the organization in a series of workshops involving around 600 people.

The role definitions that finally emerged from this process are constantly being refined. Nimmy and her team are currently reviewing the requirements for project management which can vary from assignment to assignment and in relation to whether a person is undertaking a single project or multiple projects.

The career framework drawn up by Hoskyns is backed up by personal development plans. Everybody in the organization is encouraged to maintain a personal portfolio of their achievements and career plan, including letters of commendation. Nimmy likens it to an artist's portfolio of work. Again, the emphasis is on the need to encourage people to be thinking constantly about their career. Although Hoskyns' career management and development process is always evolving, Nimmy is clearly happy with the way it has caught on at this initial stage:

'Generally, the feedback is very good. Where people are not happy it is maybe because they did not get the assignment they wanted or they think they are capable of doing X but they don't yet have the ability to get to that level. If you look at the way promotions are going and the way we are working on promotion criteria and recognition criteria, there is a real shift towards people being marketable rather than someone who can run a business unit. You get better rewarded for being a brilliant project manager than for running a bit of the business.

'The challenge is to get people management taken seriously. People-management skills vary greatly, so the challenge is to continue to improve those skills by constantly reinforcing through the culture of the organization that they are important.'

THE KEY ISSUES IN CAREER PLANNING FOR YOUR ORGANIZATION

These cases offer insights into how the issues of career management are being tackled. There is no single blueprint for how your organization should conduct its career planning. However, there are some very strong Do's and Don'ts.

Do's

- Do be very clear about your business strategy and its implications for your people. At Sun Microsystems there is a very clear recognition that organizational innovation is intimately linked to personal learning. Repeatedly we have found that asking the question, 'What kind of people do you need to fulfil your strategy?' provokes a significant reappraisal of how the organization is managing its human stocks and flows.

- Do ensure alignment of all the elements of the organization

145

with its strategy. Hoskyns clearly has a strategy of providing better service than its competitors or its would-be customers. Consequently, it seeks to hire the best – even hiring in the recession. It is committed to developing its people. It rewards its people for their contribution to the business not their position in the hierarchy. It practices openness and trust with its employees because it wants that reflected in its relationships with its customers.

- Do make explicit the values you expect your employees to exhibit. At Sun Microsystems staff are encouraged to think of themselves as being self-employed while working for the organization. Values of entrepreneurial creativity, self-reliance, independence and self-responsibility are signalled very strongly.

- Do provide employees with the opportunities to assess their preferences, their values, their skills and their development needs. Trusting employees requires that the organization ensures that all this feedback is confidential to the employee – who is free to share it with the organization if he/she so wishes.

- Do recognize that all employees are different. Creating a really dynamic developing workforce requires commitment to valuing and utilizing those differences.

- Do explain what the organization means by career management. Our experience is that interpretations of 'career management' vary widely and rarely match those of the organization. Lack of clarity generates expectations that the organization cannot or will not meet, with consequent employee frustration and disillusionment.

Don'ts

- Don't promise more than you can deliver. Career management, like marketing, is best executed by delivering more than was promised.

- Don't treat career management as an instrument of control. The aim is not to have people stay with the organization or be comfortable with it. The aim is to have the best people work for your organization to give it a competitive edge. The more

146

marketable are your people, the more productive they are. The more marketable are your people, the more potentially mobile they are. Managing those tensions is the essence of effective career management.

- Don't keep information and opinions and intentions secret. Organizations lose good people because they fail to share their intentions.

- Don't simply copy what has been done elsewhere. All organizations are unique. Their uniqueness derives from their people, their history and their culture. All of these are vital factors in career management. All must be built into the organization's approach to career management.

- Don't believe that incorporating 'People are our greatest asset' or 'This organization is only as good as its people' into your Vision or your Mission Statement means that career managment is actually happening. In a series of seminars we ran recently for a major financial institution we asked groups of managers, 'When did you last make someone better at their job?' The response, with one or two notable exceptions, was facial expressions of embarrassment, confusion and concern. When we asked, 'When did anyone last make you better at your job?' the responses included sardonic good humour, evident frustration and detectable disappointment. The reality was that they felt more pressure about short-term targets and results than about people development.

Chapter Nine
Lateral Progression

It used to be considered that sideways career moves were for those who had reached the level of their incompetence. Dr Peter, who coined the Peter Principle, facetiously called it a 'lateral arabesque'. Any individual with a history of lateral moves was regarded with suspicion. Had they been passed on from area to area in order to move a problem? The flattened pyramid has changed such thinking. If delayered organizations have made it more difficult to climb the hierarchy, one alternative involves horizontal progression. The lateral arabesque has become the corporate side-step. In today's more enlightened organizations a lateral career move can be seen as one of the ways to expand a manager's skills and knowledge and help to achieve employability. Lateral moves are a sign of flexibility and commitment not failure and exclusion.

They offer advantages both to managers and to the organizations that employ them. For managers, the opportunity to move sideways may rescue them from an outdated career choice or re-engage their interest through a new set of problems. For managers who had no particular desire to ascend to the higher reaches of the hierarchy, or doubted their abilities to do so, the pressure is now off. They can concentrate on developing their expertise or pursuing their interests through less ambitious career moves without losing face among their colleagues and friends. For those who used to believe that managerial careers were the only route to higher rewards, new options are being created. For organizations, it provides new opportunities to retain, motivate and develop those who, although not destined for the demands of higher office, can make a valuable contribution based on their knowledge and experience. It offers possibilities of retaining those whose experience of the organization and its environment are invaluable although there are no promotions available.

3M in Europe is one of a growing number of companies that is trying to dispel traditional thinking about hierarchical advancement by reassessing its attitude to lateral career moves. In the UK it recently introduced a new policy that in certain cases allows people to receive a rise in salary when they move laterally to take up a new job. Paul Davies, the company's human resource development manager for Europe, makes the point that the traditional concept that people are paid according to their position in the hierarchy and according to how many people are reporting to them, and the volume of sales they are responsible for, is becoming outmoded. He says: 'For example, you might want to put your best person into a brand new business opportunity which at the moment has almost no sales but has enormous potential and is the most complex in your organization. We have been struggling with this and continue to look at it.'

Recognizing that the rules of the game have changed and rewarding lateral moves in the same fashion as a hierarchical promotion is what Davies describes as 'putting your money where your mouth is. We need to do more in that area.'

CASE STUDY: Trent Regional Health Authority

A new approach to lateral career moves is being adopted by the National Health Service. Recent research by Roffey Park Management Institute into the effects of delayering found that the result was low morale, overwork and a feeling that opportunities for advancement were lacking. All these adverse effects have been well illustrated in the change that has taken place to transform Regional Health Authorities into Regional Offices of the NHS Executive. Observes Elizabeth Brownhill, director of personnel, Trent Regional Health Authority:

'It was agreed that the number of staff for each of the eight regional offices should be 135. This meant a considerable reduction in size, particularly for those regions where two had merged. The numbers meant that the new organization had to comprise senior, very skilled and experienced managers. This immediately reduced the traditional career prospects, particularly for middle and junior managers as well as support staff. It also meant that some staff received a big promotion, but with nowhere to progress to from the post they obtained in the new organization.

'Structures had been drawn up and within the Trent Region all posts were advertised internally to existing staff in a hierarchical cascade. With hindsight, we would avoid the cascade as this only confirmed traditional hierarchical perceptions. Another region advertised all the posts at once.'

In the new organization structure, some staff had no option other than to apply for promotion posts that would stretch their skills and some staff had to accept posts on lower grades with salaries protected. It was against this background that the NHS had been trying to gain acceptance of the notion of horizontal progression.

The traditional management career structure in the NHS used to be hospital manager, district health authority manager, regional health authority manager. The perceptions now are that a career is available in a 'provider unit' (a hospital or a management arrangement for Community Mental Health and Learning Disability Service) or a 'commissioning authority' (contracting for services from units to meet the health needs of the population of a particular area). In conjunction with Hay Management Consultants, the NHS has undertaken work to discover the management competencies inherent in the roles of chief executives of provider units and commissioning authorities. It was found that the necessary competencies are very similar, but the emphasis is different so that there is every opportunity for moving between a unit and a commissioning authority if staff wish to do so. But Brownhill stresses that this would not be hierarchical progression as previously: 'It would be seeing similar work from a very different perspective. There is no longer a management relationship between the two.'

She adds: 'One of the aims is to widen staff's knowledge base, and to this end a Regional Office Forum has been established for staff at director level and just below (about thirty staff) to enable more in-depth discussion and for people to get to know in more detail what other staff are doing. This forum also generates ideas for the organization and enables staff to test out skills, theories, ideas in a relatively safe environment. It is also teaching us a great deal about working across professional boundaries. For several people it is the first time they have been involved in something like this and the whole process is developmental for individuals.'

There are a considerable number of options for horizontal progression, in Brownhill's view, ranging from purchasing jobs to functional and specialist roles and research. 'We are attempting to equip staff with a whole range of skills which can be relevant in any of these areas together with, as far as possible, a basic technical knowledge. We have made available to staff the facility to test out for themselves the thinking on where their particular skills and aptitudes might take them, either by talking the issue through with an external consultant, occupational testing or the use of 360-degree questionnaires in association with Hay Management Consultants.'

Job descriptions for posts in the Regional Office were drawn up with key result areas and key competencies. Staff are being encouraged to explore their strengths and weaknesses in terms of competencies and to draw up a personal development plan largely based on these.

Hay Management Consultants has produced a 'resource guide' which details each competency. It includes details of what is available in terms of videos, books and training courses throughout the region and contains prescriptions for development of specific competencies. For example: read a certain book; seek these assignments; work for these mentors.

All staff are required to compile a personal development plan, both relating to their existing job and to the career moves they may wish to make in the future.

This approach is combined with more conventional ways of seeking horizontal progressions such as: secondment, part-time work, project work or short-term contract work.

Elizabeth Brownhill says: 'We are also encouraging all staff to take part in working groups which have been set up to look at various issues relating to the Regional Office, such as quality, empowerment and lateralism – one challenge is to decide what this means! Anyone at any level and from any directorate can join and make a contribution.

'We are working hard at getting people focused on operating as teams rather than in compartmentalized roles and wanting staff to be flexible in the way they work. This means learning new skills such as keyboard/computer skills or better interpersonal skills. No one working in the NHS should be without excellent interpersonal and team-working skills. Staff have to be prepared to follow a task/project

151

through on their own without relying on support for research, for example, or input in detail from senior management.

'We are trying to create a system of mentors outside the organization who not only can advise on development needs but in many cases can open up opportunities for horizontal progression.'

She sums up: 'We are aiming for staff who have skills which can be taken anywhere within the service, whatever their background; staff with sufficient knowledge of what is happening in the whole organization, not just their bit of it, to enable them to move across and rapidly develop greater depth of any specialist knowledge needed. We aim to provide staff with interesting, well-rounded roles so that they develop and have positive attributes to offer another part of the organization.'

CASE STUDY: National Westminster Life Assurance

National Westminster Life Assurance has recognized the need to redefine what is meant by career progression. Richard Crozier, the company's deputy head of group education and learning says: 'Traditionally career progression has meant climbing the hierarchical ladder step by step and the training and development required for this was, generally, quite easy to determine and implement especially when, as was often the case, the hierarchical steps were numerous and really quite small. Today, however, most organizations are moving to flatter structures – we at NatWest Life have only four levels. This means that career progression is much more likely to be lateral than vertical. We view career progression as moving from role to role within the organization whilst gaining the competencies to move up to the next level when vacancies occur.'

To identify the competencies required at each level in the company NatWest Life has drawn up a 'role profile' for each job made up of two elements:

- The main accountabilities of the role
- The competencies required to do the role (both technical and behavioural)

The company's behavioural competencies are divided into three main areas:

- Cognitive competencies
- Achievement competencies
- Interpersonal competencies

For each of the competencies there are four levels of performance. From this menu the company is able to select competencies and levels it regards as relevant to the role. This is done as a result of discussions between the job holders and their managers. Adds Crozier: 'Selecting appropriate learning styles and methodologies is not done in isolation from the company's business needs. We have devised a performance management system which assesses us against the objectives we have been set, our competencies, key accountabilities and guiding principles, and from this we determine each individual's learning and development needs. These are all linked to the business – and to individual aspirations.'

How does NatWest Life go about selecting ways to satisfy these development needs and agreeing responsibility for career progression? The company has established a culture of self-development and self-managed learning with the emphasis being very much on *self* – the individual is encouraged to take responsibility with NatWest providing the resources.

First, there is the business plan, from which all personal objectives are set. There is also the performance management system which helps identify learning needs and which assesses everyone against role profiles and the company's vision and guiding principles. At the same time, corporate requirements are examined. Is there a need to extend the competency range, for example? The company runs core competency workshops for each level of staff. These are two-day facilitated workshops which give staff the opportunity to assess themselves in a non-threatening environment against the core competencies required for their level and to feed the information gained into the personal learning and development plans.

Members of staff each have a self-managed learning workbook which helps them manage their own learning – and tells them where to get help. It contains a number of exercises such as using the Honey and Mumford questionnaire for determining their preferred learning styles.

The company also runs development centres which look at issues based around the competencies and business issues which face NatWest Life. The results of the development centres – which are

153

internally run with in-house assessors – are used to help the company as well as the individual to plan career progression by highlighting where the collective and individual strengths and weaknesses are.

The personal learning and development is reviewed on a quarterly basis. Each individual has access to a guide to developing their competencies which lists all the company's competencies – the indicated behaviours and how one can set about developing those required for any particular level or role within the company.

The company has an open learning resource centre which has up-to-date technology such as videos and CD-ROM and all the learning materials are linked to the company's competencies. This is augmented by job shadowing, job shares and projects, all of which NatWest Life has found useful in helping people to decide which direction their career might take. Crozier adds: 'Where people have identified common areas of need, we have encouraged learning sets. When we tried them first in 1992 we found staff weren't ready for them, but now they are beginning to be set up by staff themselves.'

The company also has a number of learning development advisers who act both as workshop facilitators and consultants to managers on how to guide and develop staff. They work very closely in drawing together the strands of coaching by colleagues and in-house experts. Richard Crozier says: 'Significantly, we have made a commitment to time to learn within the working day – a commitment, on average, depending on need, of up to fifteen days per annum per person. We have, in order to drive home the point that everyone is responsible for their own development, produced a video and booklet called *Making the Most of Yourself*. Everyone in the company has seen the video and has a copy of the booklet.'

NatWest has assessed the results of this approach to career progression by a combination of methods. It has an annual MORI survey and the first showed a high proportion of staff 'worried' about career progression. Since then it has held a number of course groups and produced a news-sheet outlining career progression. The most recent MORI survey showed a much reduced concern level. Adds Crozier: 'Our system for filling jobs is to let everyone apply, should they so wish, for any job vacancy or promotion which occurs – they have access to all role profiles. They can also, of course, help manage their future careers by working towards the competencies required in any job.'

Re-engineering the carrot

Any attempt to replace hierarchical promotions with horizontal progression inevitably raises the vexed question of reward systems. Neil Carr of SmithKline Beecham points out that companies traditionally pay people on a job evaluation system combined with a reward system. Job evaluation is based on job hierarchy. Adds Carr: 'The higher you are the more you get paid. All the benefits and perks are geared to the higher up the ladder you go. No organization, as far as I know, has got to the stage where people are paid for the value they add. That requires you to have a much more sophisticated system of measuring what people do and requires a lot of effort.'

In an article, entitled 'Re-engineering the carrot', published in the December 1995 issue of *Management Today*, Stuart Crainer points out that in the delayered, downsized organization, hierarchy-based reward systems are no longer relevant but the trouble is, there is no ready-made replacement.

He observes: 'The traditional pay package includes a base salary, an annual performance-related bonus, perhaps share options, as well as an array of peripheral incentives such as cars and health insurance. It remains steadfastly in place despite the best efforts of consultants (who tend to want rewards more closely tied to change initiatives), institutional shareholders (who want executives to own shares in the companies they lead) and a host of academics (who argue that companies need highly flexible packages tailored to corporate and individual needs).'

Adds Crainer: 'Wading through the theoretical mire is a daunting prospect and partly explains why the lure of the traditional package remains strong. It also explains why remuneration committees now spend days considering the possibilities rather than an hour or two after a board meeting. In fact, the more organizations examine the way they reward their executives, the more fundamental questions they are likely to encounter.'

The *Management Today* article highlights the paradox that organizations are still looking at longer-term incentives while employees' expectations no longer include life-time employment.

There is a growing body of thought that people are more interested in developing skills, enhancing their employability and being given the opportunity to manage their own careers and personal development than they are in hard cash. But Crainer is sceptical: 'The theory is neat,' he writes, 'but the profusion of articles, seminars and conferences on the subject cannot disguise the fact that it remains largely theoretical.'

Nevertheless, he cites the example of Scottish Power which emphasizes employability as a key part of its overall incentives package. Crainer notes that Scottish Power has twenty-one open learning centres offering its 8,000 employees the opportunity to develop the skills they believe are necessary, from MBAs to learning another language. Three years into the initiative, one third of employees are studying new skills and the aim is to raise this figure to 50 per cent.

Lateral Progression in Practice

For many years organizations have equated successful careers with upward promotions. This equation has been reinforced by reward systems, by internal visibility, by recognition and status. The equation has been accepted by staff, not only those who have risen to the very top, but by many below them. The difficulty facing organizations and their employees now is to change that paradigm.

Logic and facts will not be enough. Drawing attention to the consequences of delayering, exploring alternatives of staying in one job or moving through a range, offering employability not security – all of these are real but they will not necessarily change the paradigm.

The reality – as organizations are discovering – is that focusing change efforts on the individual and proposing that they take more responsibility for their own careers is not enough. Organizations have to change themselves. If hierarchy is less important, have the status symbols been removed? If lateral movements are important how will they be rewarded? If learning and development are desirable how are they rewarded and recognized? Changing paradigms requires more than providing opportunities for individuals. It demands a complete overhaul of the organization.

Chapter Ten
Managing Careers Across Borders

Our analysis has very much concentrated on UK organizations and UK operations. In reality, we are living through the emergence of global markets, including global labour markets – especially for management. In some instances globalization has opened up new career paths that offer partial compensation for the loss of career progression opportunities resulting from delayering and downsizing. Managing careers across borders places even greater responsibility on organizations to liberalize their career planning policies and to communicate to their employees the new opportunities that have become available. The trend makes it imperative for companies to develop computerized data banks recording the abilities and aspirations of their employees to ensure that when international jobs become available they can review the best internal candidates from a global pool of management talent.

Systems also need to be put in place that instantly flag up new career opportunities wherever they occur in the world. In addition, managers need help to identify whether or not they have the kind of skills that are needed in the wider international market-place. Multi-source feedback systems are among the new approaches that the more enlightened organizations are introducing to help their employees re-examine their managerial qualities in relation to the new opportunities.

Not everyone will want to jump on the international management bandwagon – and indeed many will not have the energy or the ability to cope with cross-cultural issues – and such people need reassurance that there is still a future for them inside the organization in other areas. There is also a need to give every encouragement to those employees who are inspired and invigorated by the broader vistas of international management. The information technology is now available to keep internationally-oriented managers informed about cross-border career opportunities and the more adventurous organizations are making full use of it.

Globalization demands more than the implementation of national policies on a wider canvas. Cross-cultural issues are both obstacles and opportunities for ambitious, able managers. Globalization significantly raises the costs of managing through a highly mobile management cadre. In this chapter, we review the approach and experience of two contrasting organizations. 3M has responded to globalisation by recasting its career management dramatically to encourage more cross-cultural co-operation. Standard Chartered Bank has turned away from its generalist expatriate history and traditions to foster professional localization.

CASE STUDY: 3M

In 1993 3M in Europe underwent a major restructuring. It moved from being an organization based on country units to one that was pan-European, in order to be more market focused. This set in motion a great many changes within the organization, to which its human resources (HR) division has reacted in a manner befitting a company noted for its innovative culture. One of the spin-offs of this major realignment was the appointment of Heather Bartlett as career development manager for all 3M's operations throughout Europe.

Paul Davies, 3M's manager of human resource development, Europe, believes that appointing someone to focus exclusively on career development was an innovative move probably unique to 3M in Europe at the time. Apart from the structural changes within 3M, the decision was driven by the need to focus on such issues as the flattened pyramid and 'to identify successors for the key positions in the company in the future.'

The structural changes had major implications for the way 3M managed its human resources.

As Heather Bartlett says: '3M had become increasingly attuned to the market focus. The changing market-place in Europe was moving from being country-based to being pan-European. We saw an opportunity to structure our businesses so that instead of each national unit country having all the portfolio of businesses, we set up what we have called European business centres that look at the whole European market and the individual countries have become operational arms of the central business strategy.

'That meant re-aligning a lot of resources, particularly people – but also our logistics organization and some of our other support functions, like IT and finance, so that they were aligned more closely with the businesses that were now focusing transnationally within Europe, and with stronger links directly to our parent company in the US. That had a lot of implications generally for HR practices. Previously, when all the businesses were operating within a national culture, HR practices were pretty self-contained, for legal as well as cultural reasons. They were under an umbrella of global HR strategy in terms of values and principles, but they were pretty autonomous and it became evident that once the businesses were needing to manage people in different countries from a central point, that we needed to better align ourselves in HR to make sure our policies and practices could work for everyone.'

Paul Davies adds: 'Previously, for example, everyone working for a manager in the UK was based in the UK. The appraisal process was a UK system. But overnight such a manager became responsible for eight people in eight different countries, all with different systems and procedures. It was a huge immediate change.'

Unusually, the restructuring initially had the effect of extending the pyramid rather than flattening it. The top of the pyramid was raised in terms of the number of levels available in Europe. This was because a number of new positions were created at senior levels of management within the new European organization that had previously been handled by 3M's parent company in the US. Davies describes the new organization structure that resulted as resembling a first world war German helmet. It not only created more jobs at the top but greater access for local nationals to those jobs. As Bartlett says: 'The flipside of moving those jobs to Europe was that in our parent company in the US the number of development opportunities for people going through a senior management track was reduced, so there was a shift globally in terms of where those jobs were available and we made a particular decision to try to put local nationals into those positions.

'That was a plus, but employees generally were facing some really very dramatic changes in terms of career development and the way they had always seen it. Some of the positions that used to be accessible to them in their own country were disappearing because of the centralization. Middle management jobs up to director level were now, as part of the re-alignment, becoming available on the European level, but not locally. For those people who are interested in international management and have the capabilities to do that well and are prepared to move there are greater opportunities.'

For technical and functional experts there were also exciting opportunities to expand the scope of their work to pan-European dimensions, but this did not appeal to everyone and it threw up a lot of problems concerning the need to travel frequently and spending long periods away from families. There were also issues concerning the need to work cross-culturally – understanding different behaviour patterns and mastering foreign languages. All this represented a major impact on traditional working practices at 3M. Davies points out: 'Another aspect of this has been that as this transition has gone forward, new roles are appearing that didn't exist before. It wasn't possible two years ago to predict the key roles that would become available, which made it very difficult for people to know where to aim for and how to prepare themselves. Valuing those roles has become a challenge, because traditionally evaluation was based on how many people report to you or the sales volume you are responsible for. That has given you your position in the hierarchy.'

The structural change 3M has undergone has raised questions about the efficacy of such valuation systems. As Davies points out: 'For example, you might want to put your best person into a brand new position which at the moment has almost no sales but has enormous potential and is the most complex operation in your organization. We have been struggling with that area and we are continuing to look at it. The point is that it has become much more difficult for the individual to look at and target a particular job.'

The new approach at 3M has also somewhat thrown out of gear a well-established system for ensuring that technical and functional specialists could count on career advancement without having to take on the people-handling responsibilities of general managers. According to Bartlett: 'I think the company had done a pretty good job from the 1970s really in establishing meaningful career ladders in the traditional sense of career structures which identified the opportunity for personal progression within a given function, without having to take people-management responsibility to be recognized as a manager. In fact, it was fairly pioneering in the technical community when it was first introduced. It was something that was seen as a real strength of the organization. At the end of the day, if you didn't want to be a people manager you could still see your career path in 3M if you wanted to stay with the company for around thirty years.'

The criteria by which such specialists are now evaluated are spread across the cultures of a number of countries within Europe and there is a strong need for the systems in each country to be reviewed to try to achieve more consistency.

The net result of all this change, according to Bartlett, is that employees at 3M are beginning to receive mixed messages: 'Also, a lot of people in those particular career ladders find themselves managed by people in different locations. The feeling is: "How can those managers really get to know me when they don't see what I do on a day to day basis and how can they really help me to develop my career when they're thousands of miles away and speak a very different language?"'

With so much disorienting change, 3M's HR team saw the need to break new ground and introduce policies that tackle both the needs of the new organization and the career aspirations of its employees. Says Paul Davies: 'The basis of our approach is to look at these different areas and see where there is some harmony between the needs and where there isn't. We plan to put in place processes to support both ends of the spectrum.'

This approach stops short of the more extreme concepts of employability, in which companies are expected to give their employees a free hand to upgrade their skills in areas that may be unrelated to their current work in order to improve their prospects of finding a job if and when the company decides to dispense with their services. Davies points out that in a company that makes 60,000-plus products there are very few training opportunities that could not be connected in some way to a 3M activity: 'We operate across a pretty full spectrum, but we don't go out and say: we want you to take up needlework at a manufacturing plant because we think that's a learning opportunity. If somebody comes to us with a suggestion of some development they would like to undertake that impacts an existing or future role, that's fine.'

Bartlett's initial brief on being appointed to the new role was to conduct an audit of existing career development processes across Europe. At the same time, there were moves to link up more closely with HR policies in the parent company in the US and to work in partnership with the US on improving global processes, because 'ultimately 3M is working towards not only managing its business internationally and globally but also of course all its people processes. The first priority I had was to go and talk to all the different countries and learn what their perceived issues and needs were.'

The outcome of that was the realization that there needed to be better identification of the core competencies that distinguish the management talent that 3M would need to focus its development activities on in future. The data to help isolate these capabilities was stored on separate IT systems in different countries spread throughout Europe. There was no single IT system containing the information needed for a pan-European – or global – approach, and, Bartlett adds: 'There was also the question of getting better quality data about people which encouraged us to look at the processes whereby we gather that information, which traditionally are appraisal and succession planning processes.'

It became clear that the priorities from the company's perspective were the need to initiate an information system that enabled it to handle data about its employees on a transnational basis, to improve the quality of the processes to generate that data and to focus more on development activities as a result of using that data. That meant not merely knowing who the people with potential were who were looking for further development, but also providing them with the means to do that more quickly and more effectively on an international scale.

The other side of the coin, looking at it from the employee perspective, meant focusing on what could be done to improve development initiatives so that they addressed employees' needs. An outside consultant was brought in to conduct some focus group sessions to obtain a better idea of what employees' views were.

Although 3M had not drastically cut back its headcount as a result of the restructuring, the changes were creating a high level of uncertainty among employees. Traditional rungs in the career ladder had disappeared. Heather Bartlett explains: 'If you went and talked to people in the junior levels of management, the piece they would really see is that their next level of management on a local basis had disappeared. That creates big issues for them in terms of where's the next job, because their boss is actually five or six job groups higher and in a different country. From the development point of view we had lost the traditional levels of coaches. Coaches now had to come from somewhere else, not necessarily the bosses sitting in the next office.'

The focus group work made it abundantly clear that 3M could not side-step the uncertainty and insecurity that the restructuring was causing in the minds of its employees. Says Bartlett: 'Employees, we found out from the focus group workshops, are very streetwise; they are very aware; they read the papers; they see the news; they watch what's happening to their neighbours; they know what is going on and therefore we recognize that the challenge to us in HR – and to our management – is not necessarily to try and protect them from what is going on, but to give clear messages about what the company's position is with regard to supporting them in their career development – and what the company expects from them.'

Employees recognize that they need to take more initiative to develop their own careers to ensure their future employability, but they also want to know what the company can offer to help them do that. For this reason 3M has developed a number of practical tools. The first of these was to initiate an on-line database with details about 3M's 80,000 employees around the world. Users of the system can search against a host of different criteria – language, background, experience, willingness to relocate, and so on. It was initially built up in Europe and then extended to Asia, Latin America and the US.

'It's core data,' Bartlett explains, 'so that we can offer our management better information for, in particular, candidate searching. A manufacturing manager of a plant in Germany, for example, might want to find a specialist in a particular technology. In the past he would automatically have looked in Germany. Now he will go to his HR manager and ask for the best people across Europe. We couldn't do that before other than manually telephone all our colleagues in Europe. Now we can enter the system and at least obtain a first look at our pool of talent.'

It was realized, however, that the database would only be as good as the material inserted into it. Heather Bartlett says: 'We realized that gaining credibility globally depended on the quality of what was registered on the system. So our next phase was to put a lot of effort into selling to our management the value of having a meeting once a year to review their people in a less subjective way than had perhaps been the case in the past. We offered them a framework for those meetings.'

Improvements were also made in the company's traditional

ways of looking at succession planning, which had been hugely administrative. She adds: 'It might have been useful to somebody in corporate HQ to be able to look at all these sheets of paper, but it didn't seem to give very much to local management. So we tried to shift the emphasis in the way those meetings were facilitated to be less on coding and paper-work and much more about having a valuable dialogue about people in terms of the development opportunities that can be offered.

'If we know we have all these issues, how can we constructively as a management team talk about ways that they can be handled? To be quite honest, across the world there is still a whole spectrum of how well those meetings are conducted. A lot of that is related to the appetite and skills of the leaders of particular management groups and their commitment to the process. Some are really outstanding at this and others have a long way to go. We've developed a number of tools to help them have those discussions. They vary around the world. At the moment we are still comfortable with that. As long as it works for them it doesn't have to follow a corporate edict. What we do ask of them is that they hold those meetings and we do now insist on a minimum set of outputs. These are the requirements to be able to move the process forward.'

The minimum set of outputs includes information on what 3M calls 'the health of the organization'. This is basically a snapshot of an organization's latest position – particularly related to its business situation and its strategy over the next three to five years and what the implications are for its people. Is the organization considering downsizing or making acquisitions? Does it have skill shortages in any particular area? It is principally trying to bring a closer link between the HR strategy and the business strategy. All 3M's businesses are required to report this information annually, which is then rolled up the organization.

The discussions are also aimed at identifying pools of talent within the organization. The HR department has developed a number of tools for helping organizations better identify high potential. 'To be honest,' Bartlett adds, 'a lot of it is just encouraging people to talk more openly and frankly about observable behaviours rather than simply relying on hunches – "Fred made a good presentation" or "Janet did a really good job of handling that customer."'

Davies elaborates: 'We are trying to encourage more discrimination about what is real potential as seen at this moment, because this is a regular process. So it is not forever that this judgement is made. The old bureaucratic system was to produce reams of pages of high potential, which when it came down to it were not really valid inputs.'

Up to now 3M has shied away from extensive use of assessment methodologies. Says Bartlett: 'In some countries we do have industrial psychologists as permanent members of the HR staff, but it is fairly rare. There is growing interest internally in the company to use more psychometric approaches to testing for potential, but at the moment it is fairly counter-cultural within 3M.'

Bartlett is convinced it would be dangerous to run assessment centres on a multicultural basis. Evidence from other multinational companies that 3M has benchmarked supports this view. 'The risk of cultural bias is very great. Also, increasingly from talking to experts in this area, I think we ought to be careful not to shift the pendulum from virtually no testing to perhaps doing too much of it. I am much more interested in methodologies which rely more on work sampling where we can best relate testing competencies against work-related exercises or issues.'

In 3M's experience, there are major differences in what are seen to be key competencies from one country to another. 3M's operations cover twenty-two countries in Europe and once the international HR meetings started to be held it became very evident that there was no such thing as consensus about what was a key competency. Stresses Bartlett: 'What was valued in the Nordic countries was not necessarily the same as what was valued in the Mediterranean countries. It became every evident that there were huge risks in trying to compare potential. So I think we have to introduce gradually more formalized assessments in a way that values what people see in observable behaviour within the real world – within the business scenario.'

The tool that 3M has chosen to try and make progress in this area is 360-degree feedback, using multi-source inputs. Employees receive feedback from their bosses, their peers and their subordinates. It is a technique that had already been widely used at 3M. The company had developed, with help from Ashridge Management College, its own multi-feedback tool as part of the need to improve people-management skills. 3M has been at pains to divorce the technique from traditional appraisal systems. Its prime aim now is to use 360-degree feedback for personal development – in a way that helps employees to help themselves. This is the first time 3M has used the technique to help employees in this way. Heather Bartlett says: 'We've done top-down multi-sourcing with management seeking multi-perspectives of the people below them, but we have never offered anything formal to our employees. We've encouraged them to go and seek feedback from others, but we've never offered them a tool.'

The multi-source feedback is based on core competencies. These were arrived at as the result of a project led by Paul Davies in 1994. The company decided to revisit the issue of competencies in the light of the new pan-European structure. It proved to be a challenging task. Every country in which 3M had an operation – and every function within that operation – seemed to have a different list. Management found the proliferation of competencies overwhelming. After researching different models being used internally and by other companies, plus some academic work, 3M arrived at a synthesis of generally recognized core competencies. These were then examined by a group of about forty-five 3M managers across Europe, who looked at them in terms of what they thought were the key qualities that would be required of 3M managers in the future. From that a common model was developed.

The managers who took part in the exercise were asked to relate each of the competencies, such as personal effectiveness, to someone they felt was an ideal model of that particular quality. What were the sorts of things that person did that made them very effective? Bartlett says: 'We also linked up with our colleagues in Canada, Japan, Australia and the US to check the validity of the competencies in terms of whether they would travel. Broadly speaking, the research suggests that the dimensions do travel. Sometimes the wording needs to be adapted slightly to fit the cultural interpretation.'

This gave 3M some global competencies on which to base the multi-source feedback tool it was planning to introduce. Research indicated that most companies use pencil and paper questionnaires for this kind of feedback process. They send the results to an outside organization to be processed and ideally the customer receives feedback as part of a workshop to help them handle the information thrown up. 3M decided to go a different route. A global team of psychologists and training and development people, as well as some line managers, devised a basic tool that has a set of simple behavioural statements under each of the company's core competencies. There are about thirty statements that people are asked to respond to and there are three open questions.

All the evidence was that people find the open text comments the most interesting. 'The numerical rating of behaviour is less interesting to most people,' says Bartlett, 'although it does give them a snapshot of how they are perceived – their strengths and their weaknesses. That is what we have built on. The outputs are owned by the individuals, not the company or their supervisor.

'Now the big philosophical debate inside the company with HR, line management and employees is whether it should be used as part of performance management – the appraisal system. Once it is used for that it starts to become an evaluation tool and all the evidence we have gathered from both internal and external experts is that as soon as there is an evaluation aspect people are less honest in their responses. So we are positioning it as a development tool for employees.'

To make the system more spontaneous 3M has decided to take advantage of modern electronics. Employees can use their electronic mail system to request feedback. Says Bartlett: 'That may sound somewhat impersonal, but it will help anonymity and make it more viable. Trying to get feedback from people in many different countries in a paper and pencil way is very hard to manage. The electronic system makes it almost instantaneous.'

The prototype of this system is up and running at 3M and the intention is for it to become global. Users will be able to enter information about people they are seeking feedback from and receive responses from all over the world. 'There are risks with this,' says Bartlett. 'It's a prototype and we are about to go into pilot, so we don't know whether we are going the right way or not, but I think it's been well researched and we are being very careful about the support we offer to people using it. We are going to require people to attend a workshop before they use the system so that they really understand what is behind this, what the philosophy is, what we are trying to do with it. We also want to highlight the focus on personal development and share insights that we have learned about multi-source feedback that can help or hinder its effectiveness.

'What we are aiming to do is give people greater breadth of perspective of how they are seen. The practical thing they get out of this is information about how other people see them, we hope, in a non-threatening way. It gives them data about themselves as part of the philosophy of empowerment to decide whether or not they want to do anything about this. The next support we offer is in line with when they receive the feedback. By attending the workshop, they can receive help to work on "what does this mean to me?" and "what am I prepared to do about it?"'

'The large majority of people,' adds Davies, 'will find it helpful to focus on new areas they know something about, but which they could give more attention to. There will be some cases perhaps where the information will be new and they may need more back-up.'

Bartlett says: 'We have learned from the paper and pencil tools we've used that have been well supported that this is a reasonably high-risk area and it is a very emotional area, so although we may be using an electronic tool which looks impersonal, we don't underestimate the power of what it can or can't do for people. We are very focused on supporting people when they receive the data. It is breaking new ground and our belief is the majority of people will find it useful and will benefit.'

Users of the e-mail system can select a minimum of four and a maximum of ten 'providers' from whom to seek feedback. One of them has to be their immediate supervisor. Research, mainly in the US, indicates that an average of six providers gives the best results. The data differential is usually insignificant when the opinions of more than eight providers are received. Apart from the immediate supervisor and the user's own self-assessment, all the responses are anonymous. The replies are held in an electronic holding file for twenty-one days after which a summary of the data is transmitted back to the user provided there have been at least three responses.

Although 3M has been at pains to ensure anonymity, the company accepts that the authors of open-text responses, as opposed to replies to the standard questionnaire, can sometimes be identified. But Bartlett suggests that this helps to build a more open dialogue between the participants.

Another danger is that users will choose providers whom they are fairly certain will give positive opinions, but this is less likely to be the case when the system is used exclusively for personal development and not appraisal, as is the case at 3M. Bartlett believes users will recognize the value of selecting providers who will give an honest and objective opinion. This, after all, is in the best interests of the user who is expected to make the data the nucleus of a personal development plan.

Skills workshops on how to take advantage of feedback are run at 3M to help the process. Participants receive training in how to seek, give and receive feedback and how to make practical use of it. There are also coaching workshops to encourage managers to coach their employees or peers in how to take full advantage of feedback for personal and career development.

Bartlett sees the e-mail feedback system, which can currently be operated in French, German and Spanish as well as English, helping in another area: 'An issue inside the company more broadly concerns people feeling the need to receive more recognition and not in some of the more formalized processes of awards, but just general recognition from peers and colleagues. We see the multi-source tool as offering quite an opportunity to recognize the positive contributions that people make that most of the time we never tell each other.

'So there are two sides to it. We want to use it to help build more positive recognition and we have structured it so that we are putting much emphasis on strengths and on people's potential by building on their strengths rather than necessarily getting hooked up on improving their weaknesses. Actually we don't even use the term "weaknesses". We prefer "opportunities for development".'

Once people at 3M have discovered from these processes that they have development needs, what support can they expect from the company? Bartlett says: 'Different countries are at different stages with this. Most of our countries have resources available which offer off-the-job training opportunities which are either available to employees through a paper catalogue or a computerized catalogue. Increasingly those are being revamped to offer learning opportunities under core competencies. So instead of traditionally saying: here's supervisory training, here's presentation skills, we are trying to offer these more clearly under the competencies an individual is trying to develop. Most of our countries offer different types of distance learning materials and self-learning materials. We have interactive CD facilities in some locations and many countries offer audio-tape learning packages and library resources.

'The one thing we've been missing in Europe are workshops for employees to think through a more personal development process and career development process – not necessarily because they've reached a problem situation, but just actually recognizing that they need some help thinking it through.'

169

3M's parent company in the US offers two types of workshops for this purpose. One – called a transitions workshop – is for people who, because of organizational reasons, need to change jobs. This workshop is very much focused on what the organization can offer in terms of how they can find out about vacancies, how they can improve their CVs and how they can position themselves for interviewing. The career development workshops, on the other hand, offer people the opportunity to stand back and look at their life goals and the way they are linked to their career ambitions. What does that mean to me in the new 3M?

In Europe 3M recently introduced a workshop on similar lines. It shied away from calling it a career development workshop, because that term has negative connotations in some cultures. Known simply as 'Choices', the workshop tries to give people the opportunity to look at where they are in their working lives (along the lines of Edgar Schein's career anchors). Bartlett describes the aim of the workshop as: 'recognising preferences and then helping them to think about whether they want to change anything. Maybe they don't. Maybe at the end of the experience they just realize that actually they're pretty much where they want to be. Alternatively, they may realize that they need to change direction with their career.'

Such exercises would be frustrating, of course, if managers felt that opportunities to advance their careers were dwindling in 3M. Bartlett would argue that this is not the case: 'It would be true to say that many of the opportunities that people looked for in the past in terms of hierarchical position and status are no longer available. The traditional thinking about getting your boss's job and then the job of the boss at the next level up as the way to progress your working career has definitely changed – and we say that.'

One of the ways 3M has gone about dispelling this traditional hierarchical thinking is to reassess its attitudes to lateral career moves. In the UK it recently introduced a new policy that in certain cases allows people to receive a rise in salary when they move laterally to take up a new job. Davies makes the point that the traditional concept that people are paid according to their position in the hierachy and according to how many people are reporting to them and the volume of sales they are responsible for, is becoming outmoded.

It is too early to say whether the 3M multi-source feedback system via e-mail is achieving its personal development aims, but Bartlett is optimistic: 'There are employees who are already tuned to this – you could say they're self-starters – who will do all this self-development whether 3M offers them anything or not. That's great because they will be self-sufficient. As we start to offer things like the new Choices workshop and the multi-source feedback system, we expect there will be those people who will instantly be on board with it; there will be those – and they are maybe our target group (probably 60 to 70 per cent) – who will need help but will come to accept it. Then we recognize that there will be a proportion of the population who will never really buy into this. We are working really for the majority.'

Davies regards 3M's annual organizational review as the process that will blend the needs of the business with those of the individual employee's career aspirations. 'It starts with employee inputs. You identify career discussions, areas of interest, you get feedback and if there are areas that you show a particular interest in that your manager is supportive of and is taken into the broader analysis and is accepted as a good plan for you, then it can become part of an organization's unit plan for the year. If, for example, you're in manufacturing and you want to get an opportunity in marketing and you went through that process, that opportunity would be looked for. It is much more likely to happen because of this process. It becomes a very tangible career change driven by an individual need as well as an organizational need. The two are being put together.'

Bartlett sees a fundamental shift in the new approach to career development: 'Traditionally our approaches were top down – management looking at its high potentials and judging in a relatively subjective way. It was just based on one manager's view of the people who worked for him and the employee was very remote from this. It was either done to them or on behalf of them. The shift we have made may sound fairly obvious, but it is very significant for us actually to re-engineer the process for first of all our management levels – to, in effect, make it no longer acceptable for it to be just one person's view, that we actually want broad perspectives. Having moved to broader perspectives at the management level, our next stage is to introduce the multi-source tool to the employee.'

In line with this more participative process, 3M now advertises job vacancies electronically. They are on-line and employees merely have to press PF6 on their PCs to apply for any vacancies throughout

Europe. Says Davies: 'Any day of the week you can go and look as an individual at what opportunities there are. It's another way of providing information and empowerment of the individual in this whole process.'

3M is also endeavouring to encourage participation in cross-functional project groups as a means to broaden experience and increase employability. Davies cites an example: 'In the abrasives business a particular market needed a technical person to be a project leader of a team of eight people from different functions with a very specific set of goals to be completed within an 18-month time frame. You have all the ingredients there. This wouldn't have happened without this process driving that priority up to the team's attention. They would have done it in a fairly traditional manner, giving it to the marketing manager to find the extra people.'

Adds Bartlett: 'This touches on something that will always be a challenge in our sort of complex organization – how do you marry up the needs of professional expertise within functions and the needs of cross-functional teams in the management of a business? Traditionally in 3M, people have tended to come in as specialists. They are recruited generally because of an area of skill expertise right from our PhD scientists through to a sales person who happens to have an interest in either selling into consumer or industrial markets. People come in from the functional route and it is always going to be a challenge to us. I think we believe conceptually we want to enable people to move a lot more across functions, but it is also a matter of what people want personally. Many of them will want to keep to their core area of expertise.'

CASE STUDY: Standard Chartered Bank

Like many financial institutions, Standard Chartered Bank (SCB) was plunged into deep crisis in the recession of the late 1980s. The bank's struggle for survival proved to be a catalyst for change that has swept away many of the traditions of its 160-year-old colonial heritage. Maintaining a large army of expatriates around the world was no longer viable and this drove the bank to completely rethink its corporate structure and the way it would run its foreign subsidiaries. It chose an almost diametrically opposite route to change to that adopted by 3M. Instead of expanding international career opportunities for its UK staff, it radically whittled down its cadre of expatriates from around 800 to 160. The impact on traditional career patterns within the bank was profound and it led to the bank striking a new career deal with its staff that has fundamentally changed the opportunities for advancement.

SCB is an international financial services company with a presence in over forty countries worldwide and a particular focus on emerging markets in Asia Pacific, the Middle East, South Asia and Africa. Although a predominantly British-owned bank, 90 per cent of its 26,000 employees operate in businesses outside the UK. In the past five years it has undergone a significant transformation in almost every aspect of its business.

The bank is currently in the process of moving from a predominantly British, permanently mobile, management group to one which makes wider use of local managers. This has led to the development of a global management capability and a global talent pipeline. This in turn has led to an examination of the critical skills the bank needs. Geoff Rogers, the bank's UK and Europe regional head of human resources, observes: 'Most large organizations in the international financial services industry are facing an increasingly turbulent and unpredictable market environment. The rate of product innovation is accelerating and information technology is transforming the way banks structure themselves, distribute and tailor their services. These changes are bringing new challenges to the risk/reward trade off. Globalization and government deregulation are also changing the nature of competition and the needs and wants of corporate and retail customers.'

Until recently the term 'international manager' at SCB applied solely to members of a closely knit group of mainly British managers who were almost permanently mobile and occupied many of the key roles in a federation of businesses across the world. The bank sees the role of the new international manager as something that involves a broader definition: A manager who primarily lives and works in his home country, but who becomes part of an integrated international business network through:

- induction and international training
- international conferences and meetings
- regular cross-border network contact – personal and electronic
- short-term cross-border projects

173

- a limited number of international appointments to develop critical experience/skills

Rogers adds: 'This broader definition is partly driven by the increasing difficulty we are experiencing in enabling cross-border postings and the cost of such movement. The new international manager also requires a different set of skills which are oriented towards managing in a flatter cross-border network.' In particular, the critical skill areas of SCB have been:

- strategic perspective – understanding the global and local environment
- influencing skills to operate in an integrated, less hierarchical network
- tolerance of the ambiguity involved in managing across an international network where managers often have responsibility without authority
- cross-cultural management skills

Recruiting and developing managers with these skills continues to be one of the most significant constraints to the development of the bank's business.

Geoff Rogers observes that moving managers around the world is only one of the tools to develop global management capability and that it is becoming increasingly difficult and expensive. The net additional cost of 380 international assigned managers at SCB is £26 million a year. The local nationals the bank most wants to move (those from Asia Pacific) are reluctant for understandable reasons – ties with the 'extended family' and the absence of suitable cultural/educational support systems away from home base.

Standard Chartered has therefore had to make use of a range of tools designed to internationalize local managers, other than by cross-border assignment. Among the specific tools it has introduced are the following:

- *Corporate induction.* For all new recruits; it reflects both a global and local strategy, culture and values.

- *International Graduate Recruitment.* The bank actively recruits Asians and Africans who have been educated in Europe and the US for employment in their 'home' country.

- *Graduate Entry Training.* Fast-track graduates, drawn from international and local universities, are inducted at a single global training centre for the first six months before being appointed to home country roles. This includes a three-month international project assignment.

- *Global Talent Bank Management.* The bank has established a global talent bank for which it actively monitors the development of over 150 managers across the group's businesses.

- *International Education.* A range of globally managed international business education programmes have been introduced. These include:
  International Management Programme
  (INSEAD Euro-Asia Centre)
  Global MBA – 60 students from 20 countries
  (Henley Management College)
  International Consortium programmes (INSEAD and LBS)

Says Rogers: 'None of these methods is unique to Standard Chartered, but they have all been implemented in response to the need to develop local managers with the skills and experience to manage in an international network.'

Fundamental change
The market forces that have impacted on SCB have resulted in fundamental changes throughout the whole organization, not merely in its approach to the management of foreign subsidiaries. Until the late 1980s the bank was still being run according to the traditions of its colonial heritage. A cadre of 800 mainly British expatriates filled all the key roles throughout the group. Whittling that down to a hard core of around 160 permanently mobile expatriates has brought about a very significant change to the pattern of careers within the bank. It has also thrown wide open the pool of people who can aspire to the highest levels in the organization. In the past, top jobs were confined pretty much to an élite group of people whose length of service and broad experience of expatrate management were their passport to reward. Today the emphasis is on promoting local managers. As Geoff Rogers says: 'The glass ceiling is still there to be honest. The most senior levels still mainly comprise Anglo-Americans, but you can see the ceiling moving up all the time in terms of local content.'

175

At the same time, SCB has reduced the number of job grades within the bank and is planning to reduce them still further. This is having a significant impact on promotion opportunities and managers increasingly need to view their development in terms of horizontal development. In addition, the bank has taken radical steps to introduce new blood to broaden its perspectives. Some 50 per cent of the top 400 people who were running the bank in 1990 have been replaced by managers from other organizations.

Rogers explains that this policy has exploded the traditional notions of how people rose to the top of SCB: 'Until recent years nobody would have been promoted to a senior level unless they had been in the bank for twenty years or more and they had been through all the grades and had been out in the overseas network. That is no longer the case and it has led to a fundamental change in terms of recruiting new people. We now believe that management development begins with recruitment: that is, recruiting the right people in the first place.

'The reality was that the bank was in crisis. If we could have anticipated these changes over a five-year period we could have developed and re-oriented people, but it was a question of survival and that was the first priority of the bank – to survive as a business and it's done that very successfully as the profits and performance have shown.'

The other major change that Rogers has witnessed in his five years with the bank is the trend towards greater professionalism. 'To be quite honest, in the late 1980s there were a lot of gifted amateurs around in steady state markets with a fairly assured profit stream. It was all about who you knew and there was no need for much creativity, innovation or flexibility. It was a steady state environment and a protected regulatory environment in each country. So you had a very cosy cartel. There was no competition until international financial services were deregulated in many of the territories where SCB operated. This happened in some countries over a relatively short time period.'

He goes on: 'In the past the senior management were generalists who had been in every bit of the bank – probably started on the telex machine – and their experience and core competencies were a collection of countries. Now that experience is not nearly as important as the vertical slice – in other words, having a professional expertise in corporate banking or international trade finance or markets and treasury. Because our competition has become that much more sophisticated, our managers need to move from being a general banker to being more specialized. We still have a need for a general management cadre at the senior level, but the balance has moved from the generalist banking career now to more professional specialism. Those who are really good professionals but also have the necessary leadership and multicultural skills will now fill the key roles.'

However, Rogers believes it is going to be increasingly difficult for people to make long-term career plans: 'There are some people who clearly have plans and their influence skills are such that they can achieve those plans. But I would say that being able to forecast what job roles, content and competencies are going to be much more than three to five years out is now impossible. Every day key business areas are redesigning jobs, the competency sets that are required, and probably the real growth products and markets we need to be in haven't even been invented yet.'

The sort of choices people at SCB are now able to make are: 'Do I want to be a product specialist and focus down on this particular career stream or do I want to be a business manager with a more generalist skill, where I need to gain a portfolio of experiences in terms of products and markets?' In the latter case, it means becoming more mobile and more flexible. Adds Rogers: 'There are more unknowns, but potentially the opportunities are greater even if the risks are higher. So I would say: if you want to follow a general management career and you want to be a business leader, you need to have a broader experience. You need to have a firm anchor somewhere in one of the business segments, but your risks are going to be higher in terms of where you go, when you go and what you are prepared to do. Potentially the rewards are higher because you've built a portfolio of skills that you are prepared to manage in the unknown.

'It's managing careers in the unknown and that's about building a set of capabilities. It is not about specific career plans and succession plans.'

It also, of course, requires the organization to be forgiving when those who take risks are not as successful as expected. Rogers believes people's careers will revolve on the kind of reputation they build up for being professional and adventurous:

'With tighter budgets and head count management, increasingly it is your professional reputation and your personal network that will count most. People will fight to find a job for those who are in a business where opportunities have shrunk provided they are valued, have made a contribution and have a good personal network.'

New Deal
SCB has begun to strike a new deal with its employees which takes account of the impact of change on traditional career paths. It recognizes that in the new circumstances a paradox has to be addressed. Most organizations now identify people as their key source of competitive advantage because people cannot be readily duplicated by rivals, whereas technology and branding, for example, can. But the old relationships between the individual and the employer are breaking down; traditional career ladders are falling away; individual loyalty is to one's own career rather than to the bank; in a flatter organization people's careers plateau at an earlier stage.

Observes Rogers: 'In particular, organizations now have fewer layers, meaning that employees will no longer receive frequent periodic promotions up a narrow grading scale. Many employees will reach a level at an early stage beyond which promotion is unlikely.

'Arising from a perception of limited opportunities and lack of employer loyalty, capable employees now tend to regard themselves as highly mobile between organizations, seeking opportunities that enhance their CV, from whichever source these may originate. This phenomenon can be seen in the wider employment market and presents a particular challenge to SCB.'

Various factors have combined to make the traditional career ladder steadily less relevant in SCB:

- changes in the business focus of SCB
- restructuring
- the drive for greater efficiency and better ways of working
- changes in the attitude of the bank towards its workforce
- changes in employees' attitudes to their careers, driven by changes in the wider working environment.

SCB has identified a number of barriers that need to be overcome to ease the path towards successful implementation of a new approach to career management. They require the bank to:

178

Resolve:
- dual career and re-entry issues
- lack of clarity over succession planning and career movement processes
- functional reward barriers to cross-functional movements
  the concerns of older staff over 'employability'

Identify:
- high potential staff early and effectively
- key development roles
- functional career paths and bridges between them
- ownership of career management within the bank

Change:
- existing mind-sets on lateral moves, projects and attachments
- attitudes of people halfway up the ladder

Encourage:
- good people to take career risks and managers to accept them
- desired behaviours and moves without lifting the lid on costs
- managers to share their high potential staff
- international experience at an early age
- longer-term perspectives on career and reward structures

Some of these issues have long been familiar to SCB, but others are assuming greater significance, such as geographic mobility of staff whose spouses also have a demanding career. Further issues arise directly from the changes that are taking place in the company. For example, older staff may not welcome the new deal when they perceive the external employment market as one that discriminates on the basis of age. Staff who have climbed part way up the old ladder may feel the removal of the ladder undermines their past achievements.

A career for life is not ruled out at SCB, provided staff realize that they need to approach career planning from a different perspective. 'I tell people they can have a job for life,' says Rogers, 'but they have to realize that they may have to change that job inside SCB several times. If you re-skill yourself, you are constantly aware of where the new product developments are and you are on the wave of that change, the opportunities are there. Get involved in that project which is leading-edge and you have got a good chance of being continously employed by SCB. I have no doubt about that.'

The new deal for the employer/employee relationship at SCB

involves some changes in process but is principally a shift in mind-sets. It involves swapping the mentality of employment, promotions and status for the new values of employability, experience and personal satisfaction:

	Old Understanding	**New Deal**
Relationship	Parent–child	Adult–adult
Offer of	Lifetime employment	Ongoing employability
Progress means	Regular promotions up a grade scale	Continued opportunities for development, contribution and reward
Recognition comes from	Avoiding mistakes	Adding value
Career is owned by	The bank	The individual
Success equals	Senior jobs with visible status	Meeting personal career goals
Career paths are	Relatively fixed	Co-determined and fluid
Individual needs and wants are	Not particularly important	Matched to those of the bank wherever possible
A career is	A ladder	An expanding experience matrix

SCB defines career management as: 'A partnership between the individual and the Group in which people are encouraged to maximize their potential in order to develop the business'.

The new deal, says Rogers, represents a move away from the old corporate planning, but does not abandon staff to manage their careers on their own. Instead, individuals are encouraged to articulate their own career goals and the bank provides tools and techniques that will help them achieve these in a way that maximizes business success.

Under the new deal, the bank has identified various tools and opportunities that it wishes to offer every employee as its part of the bargain. These include development measures that will enhance both current performance and the individual's internal and external employability:

- *Training* to perform effectively in the current job
- *Opportunities* to grow through challenging work assignments
- *Experience* that maintains or increases employability

- *Environment* that encourages continuous learning and development
- *Adaptability* skills to withstand a changing environment
- *Cross-functional moves* for development reasons or on reaching a plateau
- *Fair remuneration* for current performance
- *Dialogue* and negotiation regarding career aspirations
- *Tools and Techniques* to assist career management
- *Focus* on outputs and learning rather than inputs
- *Balance* of work and personal needs

Some staff have been identified by the bank as having high potential for undertaking senior management roles in the future. For these staff the bank offers additional opportunities, most of which have a longer-term perspective, intended to encourage the individuals to remain with the bank and maintain a high level of contribution. The offers to high-potential staff include:

- Preparation for the next job and beyond
- International assignments
- Reward systems that encourage a longer-term relationship
- Systematic career review processes

The individual's side of SCB's new deal reflects a proactive stance towards management of his or her own career. However, there needs to be a degree of pragmatism and recognizing the constraints of reality. Whilst the bank encourages individuals to articulate career wishes, the extent to which these can be fulfilled inevitably needs to be viewed in the context of business needs. What the bank expects from its staff is the following:

Our People Should	But . . .
Manage their own careers	In partnership with the bank
Identify personal career goals	Remain flexible and open-minded
Share career goals openly	Understand the bank's business needs
Seek personal development opportunities and career moves	Be realistic and respect the needs of current assignments
Perform to high standards	

Above all, the bank expects to change the perception of what it means to 'get on' by replacing an appetite for promotion with a hunger for opportunities to *develop, contribute* and be *rewarded*.

The ultimate career aspiration of staff at SCB identified as having high potential will primarily be shaped by two factors under the new deal: their geographic mobility and their willingness to change business or function. These factors reflect the bank's need to have senior managers with an international perspective and a broad understanding of its range of business. Those members of staff who successfully show flexibility in both contexts can realistically aspire to the most senior general management positions.

The bank has set out the basic steps for developing a career plan, recognizing that many of its employees will not have been used to thinking about their career on a proactive basis. The first step, it suggests, is often the hardest:

Step 1: Establish career and life goals
Step 2: Develop a personal profile (including strengths and weaknesses)
Step 3: Identify past achievements and significant learning events
Step 4: Seek the views of others
Step 5: Analyse the present situation and identify the future picture
Step 6: Map a self-development route from the present to the future

In addition, the bank has identified key principles that underpin these six steps. The essential message they convey is the development and maintenance of flexibility in skills and outlook:

- Establish career aims in terms of role types, not specific jobs
- Value lateral moves, projects, attachments and other learning opportunities
- Think creatively about different paths to a target role
- Seek opportunities for cross-functional and cross-border experience
- Develop core competencies and generic skills
- Maintain a fall-back plan in case initial goals need to be changed

The bank is creating a substantial armoury of tools to help its staff to assess, develop and maximize their own potential:

- Assessment centres
- Executive development counselling
- Mentoring and coaching
- Competency framework
- Personal development plans
- Management development and technical training frameworks
- JobWatch to create an internal talent market
- High potential lists maintained by each business and function
- 80/20 target – i.e. to fill senior vacancies 80 per cent internally, 20 per cent externally

There is a still a long way to go before these measures are operating at grass roots level across SCB, but the bank believes that collectively they should ensure a sufficiently strong pipeline of talent to achieve its key resourcing goal of filling 80 per cent of senior vacancies from within. The remaining 20 per cent of vacancies will continue to be filled by external recruitment, which refreshes the bank's talent pool through the introduction of new skills and perspective.

A set of core managerial capabilities have been identified at SCB. Demonstration of these capabilities to a high level will mark out senior managers of the future:

- Strategic perspective
- Business goal management
- Customer focus
- People management
- Multicultural awareness
- Networking
- Change agent
- Information systems management
- Risk management

Each capability comprises several specific competencies which can be displayed at various levels. Jobs in the bank are increasingly described in terms of the level of each competence that successful performance requires.

The bank is exploring a variety of other support facilities to help staff plan their careers more effectively. They include self-assessment centres, career 'health checks', cash incentives for lateral and cross-functional career moves and job rotation programmes.

SCB has spent around two years exploring the different options for making its staff more career-resilient and has plans in 1996 to be more proactive in introducing the new deal programme. Geoff Rogers accepts that the new approach will cause some anxiety in the bank: 'It does in some ways raise anxieties understandably in people who have been in protected areas who have really not felt the turbulence, because there are businesses and areas which have gone through all the change fairly smoothly. They are successful businesses in a growth market and even those areas are now being impacted.'

The initial target groups for getting the message across have been the bank's MBAs and its graduate recruits. It has around 60 MBAs on an internal distance learning programme run by Henley Management College, but career development needs are not confined to senior and high potential managers. In the UK, secretaries have turned out to be another priority group. Workshops have been set up to help them understand more clearly how the role of the secretary is changing and the necessary steps for adopting career self-management.

The workshops are SCB's response to growing concern among secretaries that they are at the heart of many of the technological changes that are sweeping the bank and yet there were no programmes to specifically address their needs. Rogers acknowledges this:

'The reality is that secretaries have been at the hub of the technology drive. In the five years I have been at the bank we've literally gone from faxes being new to global e-mail and Lotus Notes and secretaries virtually becoming administrative managers running budgets, global e-mailing and putting sophisticated presentations together. Increasingly, they now have opportunities to get into junior management roles because they've become information managers. In fact, information manager is now a better description for most of the secretaries.'

To address this issue, SCB has set up a career planning working group made up of secretaries. Nobody is more aware than they are of the extent to which their jobs are changing and that they are therefore in the best position to decide what the priorities are. The bank has promised to provide the support and development that they conclude is necessary for the new climate.

The processes SCB has put in place to take account of its need to offer a new deal to its managers and staff are still at the experimental stage. Only time will tell if they are working and providing people with the opportunity to re-assess and re-align their careers in the changed circumstances imposed on the bank as the result of a fast-moving market-place. The detailed efforts the bank has made to ensure that it is well equipped to cope with the challenges it will face up to the end of the millennium and beyond are a measure of its determination not to allow events to overtake it.

Chapter Eleven
The Nomadic Manager

To ensure employability, ambitious managers will increasingly have to become nomadic, moving from project group to project group, from job to job and from company to company, to update their knowledge and broaden their skills. It is quite likely they will eventually find themselves part of a virtual organization with no definite home base. Just as the nomads of old had no permanent address and roamed from place to place in search of sustenance to ensure their survival, the career-minded manager will journey across a corporate landscape that is unforgiving and constantly changing, so that the old maps are not only useless but dangerous. As one senior HR manager put it, it is no longer correct to talk about career paths. The term should be 'career journey' because it is a continuing voyage into the unknown.

At the same time all the conventional perceptions of the relationship between employer and employee will undergo radical change. Organizations can no longer offer job security. They are struggling to find something to put in its place, but increasingly employers and employees will find themselves having to face inevitable divorce. By the same token, managers will need to become more adventurous, constantly alert to the next potential career move, whether it is inside or outside the organization they currently work for. Organizations are making brave attempts to support employees in their quest for employability. In return, managers are expected to show a degree of loyalty while they remain in the organization, however short a period that may be. But nobody any longer will blame managers for keeping a weather eye open for the career move that will take them to another organization. If the marriage vows are no longer sacrosanct, adultery should not be regarded as a sin.

There are already signs that corporate life is moving in this direction in the UK. At Mercury Communications, the Cable & Wireless-owned telephone company that has taken on the mighty BT, on average employees are in their low thirties and they stay less than two years with the company before moving on. Managers generally stay less than five years with the company. The average employee works less than a year under the same boss.

Steve Harrison, 3M

Few managers would claim that they had a master plan when they set out on their careers and that they have stuck to it rigidly. When most of today's managers launched their careers, there was nothing like the pressure to seek employability as opposed to employment. The pace of change was nowhere near as rapid. Information technology was not the force for change that it is now. Job insecurity, in so far as it existed, was only a problem for manual workers. As we have argued consistently through this book, environmental turbulence and organizational change have proved to be catalysts for major shifts in approaches to careers.

However, ambitious managers seem often to have an intuition and an instinct for making the right career moves at the right time in order to advance their causes. When their careers are analysed their career paths seem to have been dictated more by serendipity than by scientific planning, but instinctively they seem to recognize the changing times and what they mean in terms of furthering their careers and maintaining their employability. A case in point is Steve Harrison, an abrasives product manager with 3M UK. At thirty-one, his current job involves him in assessing the market needs of 3M's abrasives products for the automotive trades throughout Europe and the Middle East. He spends much of his time liaising with technical staff at 3M to ensure the right products are being developed to support marketing campaigns.

Harrison would never have dreamed, when he first set out on his career, that he would end up in marketing. It seemed much more likely that he was destined to spend all his working life on the technology side or in production. He left school at sixteen with just three O levels and, acting on the advice of his parents, took up an apprenticeship as an electronic technician with BICC, the leading UK-based cable-maker. Harrison spent 'five quite happy years' with the firm. He found the work a valuable experience, operating under a strict disciplinarian who demanded high standards of performance, while at the same time mixing with bright graduates who had been hired to develop computerization and automation at the company.

'When I went for the interview at BICC,' he says, 'the idea of undertaking further education never occurred to me, to be honest. I thought my education was all over by then. It was a question of: "that's all behind me; show me what you want me to do".'

When, however, Harrison learned that an old school friend had gone to university and was doing well, he decided to follow suit. At twenty-one he put a temporary stop to his career to take a degree at Sheffield University, but wasn't immediately convinced that he had done the right thing: 'I went to university in 1985 and for two years I really thought it was the worst mistake I had ever made. It was the boom time and at 21/22 you saw all your friends making money. If I had stuck with my job I would have been upgraded and I would have left home and bought a flat and participated in the boom. Seeing everyone else doing well while you are studying is rather depressing. So I was quite pleased when the recession came along! Without it I wonder if I would have made up the lost ground. It's very difficult when you are twenty-two to take the long view.'

After attaining his degree, Harrison realized he was 'going to come out at the end of the pipeline as a high-skilled electronic engineer, which was not what I had set out to do. I was too focused on one area. So I went to Cranfield and did a master's degree in computer-integrated manufacturing'.

The Cranfield degree broadened Harrison's experience. He now felt he knew a lot about something (electronic engineering) and something about a lot of things. He went to Cranfield under a scholarship from Ford and it seemed a foregone conclusion that he would join the car company to build his career. However, while at the business school, he carried out a lot of research into what companies have to offer and he was particularly impressed by articles he read about 3M which described it as highly innovative and a company that had a caring culture. The company's values, as described in the articles, appealed to him.

He joined 3M as a process engineer. It appeared to be an exciting time to work for the company since it planned to introduce advanced computer techniques for automating production lines, which Harrison felt would broaden his experience still further. But the computerization took longer to develop than Harrison had reckoned. He felt his career was dragging to a halt and soon became impatient for some new action.

Team-working was being introduced in the abrasives division of 3M, which involved a fundamental switch from the old-style autocratic management approach. A production job opened up within this new operating procedure and Harrison seized the opportunity. Working in the team environment proved to be 'quite hard and painful, but we did it in a democratic way'. Eventually he adapted and moved to another part of the same plant to repeat the exercise.

It wasn't long, though, before Harrison's ambitions were driving him on again. He admits that there was still no master plan, just the intuitive feeling that the time was right to make another move: 'My analysis would be that I basically get itchy feet. I'm a bit of a roamer. You may as well make it a virtue.'

By now the way ahead was becoming a lot clearer to Harrison. The experimental team-working had opened his eyes to new possibilities and it began to make him think about how the future of management was likely to evolve to his advantage. He did not see his current job as being the vehicle that would place him at the leading edge of new management processes. 'I don't think the plant manager of the future will be a production man who has come up through industrial engineering. He will be a business manager.

'The qualities, I would suggest, a plant manager or business manager will need are a good understanding of the product, processes and people and a good understanding of the business. That suits me well. What I found when I moved across into marketing was that there are a lot of other jobs I had no idea about.'

So Harrison made the brave switch from a technically-oriented production job to one that supports the marketing of products all over Europe and the Middle East. He does not claim to be the only person to have made such a dramatic change of direction in his career, but he doubts if many have done it at such a young age.

The move was not made without a certain amount of difficulty. First of all, there was the insecurity of moving from 'somewhere where I felt quite comfortable and was probably quite effective to somewhere where I knew nobody and knew nothing about the job.' At the same time, Harrison had leap-frogged over a number of people who had been following the traditional route up the hierarchical 'chimney' and who understandably resented this interloper from a production background who had no business to be in marketing. Harrison describes it graphically as being 'like the body rejecting a transplant'. He suspected that there were plenty of people who would have relished the idea of seeing him fall flat on his face in the alien environment. 'If there is any single lesson to emerge from the experience, it is that if you are going to do something like that, the process has to be handled properly. I'm relatively mature in my outlook and I was prepared to put up with it, but the culture of the company has to be one that says people are expected to hop around the different functions. If the culture says, "this is your chimney and you've got to climb up it" and there are these air-raids going on from time to time, it can be quite destructive.'

In hindsight, Harrison is philosophical about what happened. 'I have no real problem with it now. There was a gap and the people in line to fill that gap were not perceived to have the right skills' set to do it. Serendipity was served, I guess, because I was looking for a move and the company was looking for someone. I guess it decided to take a calculated risk.'

There is no question that Harrison, who has spent six years at 3M, is a man in a hurry. 'You look at people who have reached a senior level and you think to yourself, "I aspire to that, but not at the age of fifty-five. I want to be playing golf by then." That's almost my dilemma now. I have got the next two or three years or so and it is either up or out. If there were a master plan it would be to finish early. There is no point pretending you're satisfied when you are not. Your actions will belie the truth.'

Harrison admits that he did not find the fundamental switch from production to marketing an easy ride. 'I certainly examined my belief in myself a number of times. It was quite humbling.' His instinct in the first six months of the new job was to let discretion be the better part of valour. 'I was determined not to make a mistake. I was much more conservative than is natural for me. It opened me up to the criticism that I did not act very rapidly. I chose to take that criticism because I didn't want to make any mistakes and fall flat on my face. There was this big fear of an arm going around my shoulder after about a year and someone saying: "We had better pull you out. We knew it was going to be a tall order when we offered you the job and you've proved we were right!" In the second six months I started to open up and share my observations.'

Serendipity has served Harrison well, but the message has not escaped him. For the shrewd, career-minded executive there is often a common thread that combines self-interest and the interests of the organization. Being constantly alert to such opportunities is the art of being career-resilient. There is little doubt Harrison will keep a weather eye open for the common ground in future and that he will use that as his route to career advancement.

Mandy Johnson, SmithKline Beecham

Mandy Johnson, UK graduate recruitment manager at SmithKline Beecham (SB), is another person who cannot claim to have organized her career according to a detailed master plan. However, in her eleven years at the leading pharmaceutical company, she has made a series of moves aimed at broadening her experience base and gaining greater insight into the different aspects of running a major corporation. She has turned down several career options that did not meet with these ambitions and is happy to move sideways if it is likely to enhance her experience and visibility. She says: 'Whilst I admire people who have an overall master plan for their careers, I've seen some people with such master plans but not the talent to achieve them and I've seen how disappointed and upset they have become when they couldn't achieve what they set out to do. Every experience I have had I have enjoyed and got a lot out of it.'

Johnson joined SB as a graduate trainee pharmaceutical sales representative from London University. She may not have had a master plan, but she had a very definite role model in mind when she took the job: 'I wanted to join a blue-chip company. My father had been with Esso for years and had developed a fabulous career, having started in sales. That looked like a good role model for me. I also had a friend who had done the same degree as me and had joined a pharmaceutical company and was really enjoying it.'

She was clear in her mind that she wanted to be in sales even though there is evidence to suggest that women are more suited to marketing and meet with less male chauvinism in that function. 'I think you can find chauvinism wherever you want to. At the moment we have a 50/50 mix of men and women in the pharmaceutical sales force, although that was not the case when I joined.'

Being part of a sales force selling prescriptive drugs to general practitioners and hospital doctors appealed to Johnson partly because it meant putting her degree in physiology to good practical use. 'In those days there was a tendency to look very much for something where you thought you would be able to use your degree. My degree did give me a head start with the training to be a medical rep because I knew the necessary background in anatomy, physiology and pharmacology and had an understanding of disease processes.'

The first career switch was to be three years later when Johnson became a sales training officer. This was a very deliberate move and was again inspired by a role model. Getting into training was a dream that was planted in Johnson's mind almost from the first day of her own initial training course. 'I saw qualities in my training officer which I would have liked to have had myself. I saw how much I had grown and developed and how much I had got out of the course. I thought – rightly so – it would be marvellous to be in a position to have some input into people's growth and development. I had never had any problem with standing up in front of a room full of people. I didn't have any shyness about dealing with a group of people. I found that quite exciting.'

It might be argued that in terms of Edgar Schein's career anchors, Johnson had found the key to her job motivation, but she describes the move simply as 'a sensible next step'. She also denies that it was inspired by raw ambition, but the rudiments of a career path were clearly already beginning to occur to her. 'I wasn't without ambition. I wasn't just a jellyfish floating around, but I was not somebody who yearned to end up leading a company. I did feel I didn't want to stay a medical rep for ever and the training officer who trained me when I joined went on to do great things, which again provided a model for me. A lot of people went from sales training into regional management. It was always going to be a good option to follow.'

Johnson's instincts proved to be well-founded. Within a year she was headhunted internally to be a regional manager running a team of sales representatives. That was in 1989, a year after the SmithKline Beecham merger. Again, it was the answer to a prayer: 'That gave me people management, which is what I wanted. If you spend a significant amount of time in the field, which I did, you also have credibility. I knew if anyone tried to pull the wool over my eyes I would probably be able to spot it. I did that job for four years and I really enjoyed it, but I also felt I wanted to try something different. Potentially I could have moved on and upwards, but although people say I'm ambitious, my main concern is doing a job where I am challenged and feel I can add value.'

In 1992 she became a marketing researcher, a lateral move, which someone else so well-placed on the corporate ladder might have been reluctant to take on. It fitted into Johnson's desire to broaden her experience very neatly, however: 'I don't have a particular status fixation. I'm very keen on growing and developing. I want to broaden my skills base. I wasn't sure that my quantitative skills were as strong as they could be and I wanted to change jobs because I had been a regional manager for nearly four years. There wasn't an obvious next step on the sales ladder except as a national sales manager, which would have meant managing others again and if I went down that route it would have narrowed me. Market research was something that would grow and develop me and give me the opportunity to see what it was like to work in head office, have a look at marketing and discover what other opportunities there might be for me.'

In the light of recent developments in the economic climate and its impact on jobs, it would be easy to deduce that Johnson was being shrewd and proactive, but she says that if she had any preoccupation at the time it was not to allow her horizons to become too narrow. The fact that this is now regarded as the main instrument of remaining employable was not uppermost in her thoughts at the time. She also admits that making bold changes in her career was in itself something that gave her a sense of excitement: 'I really see the benefits of doing it rather than finding it threatening.'

The next move was into product marketing, where she was given the opportunity to launch a new prescription drug. 'It was the first launch worldwide, so it was fairly high profile, but there were a lot of people to hold my hand. It was a brilliant job.'

In October 1995 Johnson was approached and asked to apply for her current job in graduate recruitment. At last it meant a promotion. 'I was a regional manager at the age of 26, which was relatively young and then I had done sideways moves into marketing research and product management, so I did feel it was about time I went up a notch. It took me out of the UK pharmaceutical business and into the bigger SB, something I was really interested in because I had spent all my career in one part of SB. I thought it would be great to see other parts of the company. For example, there is consumer healthcare, which is a huge sector, to which I had had no exposure. I now work in corporate management development, which means working as part of a transatlantic team, something I had never done before. I have responsibilities which to a degree stretch across Europe.'

Several strands of Johnson's career have come together in the latest job. She is again involved in training and development and she also argues that there is a strong sales and marketing element to the work. 'I'm selling SB to the graduates and I'm selling my product, which is those people, to my internal client base. I'm measured by my products. You have to know what your customer needs are. The more I do it the more I realize how strong the sales element is. It's wonderful. It gives me a buzz.'

Master plan or not, there has been a lot of logic to the career path Johnson has followed. 'I've made sure there has been logic. I've looked at lots of other options along the way and I have only taken steps I felt were sensible. I have turned down jobs where I didn't think it was a logical step to take.'

She has already mapped out her next career moves. High on the priority list is a return to marketing. She is concerned that if she stays in a corporate function for too long she will lose the credibility of her line management background. Again, she is determined not to narrow her options by becoming typecast as someone who works in the human resource function.

Her spell in graduate recruitment has certainly helped to enhance her visibility. She runs an MBA intern programme, which involves meetings with top management at SB. She has also worked on a top management presentation about the company's current graduate and MBA recruitment strategy and how it could be improved, which has again helped to enhance her credibility and visibility.

Working in a staff function has underlined the differences between such roles and performing a line management job. 'When you're in the line you're doing something very tangible and you are measured on that. It's a bit woolly in HR and it can be extraordinarily frustrating. It's shown me that it is extremely important to have influencing skills, customer focus, qualities you learn from other jobs. It has given me a better understanding of the big picture.'

All change

Both Harrison and Johnson managed to broaden their career base significantly and enhance their employability while staying within one company. It signifies their high degree of awareness of the opportunities for doing so and their companies' flexibility in making such fundamental job switches possible. But research commissioned by GHN, the London-based specialists in coaching and mentoring for senior managers, indicates that many companies do not provide adequate support for executives wishing to make role switches. The research also identifies a major discrepancy between what personnel directors and role-changers think motivates people to accept a role change. For role-changers the most important factor is the opportunity for career development. Also cited are skills enhancement and increased employability. Personnel directors, on the other hand, cite job challenge as the main motivator along with increased remuneration, recognition and status.

This confirms our view that Nomads – and both Johnson and Harrison have demonstrated nomadic qualities – have different values from Palm Trees (see Chapter Two). Personnel directors, judging by their beliefs about motivational factors, may well be Palm Trees. Many organizations are still operating within mind-sets that assume jobs for life, upward progression, narrow specialization with its technical challenges and financial rewards based on experience and seniority. Such mind-sets are inappropriate to current turbulent environments and fail to reflect the values of many employees. In particular, they do not match the needs of those employees most likely to respond appropriately to the changing circumstances of career management. There is an urgent need for organizations to survey their employees and prospective employees to identify their values and interests. Only with up-to-date information can organizations hope to design and implement effective reward systems and career management policies. Relying on outdated stereotypes risks losing the organization's best people to more responsive rivals.

The research found that companies are not providing appropriate support to help senior executives manage change positively. In the majority of corporate cultures 'it is still not OK to ask for help' and almost a quarter of role-changers were offered no support. What is available is often very traditional and not tailored to meet individual role-changer needs. Only 7 per cent of companies questioned provide a specific role change programme. Nearly half the role-changers felt they could have made an earlier contribution to the bottom line if they had received a tailored role change programme.

The research was conducted in the summer of 1995 and looked at the effects of role change among a selection of *Times Top 1000* companies. Some 109 personnel directors and forty-five senior executives who had changed roles in the last two years participated in the survey. The research was directed specifically at senior managers, earning in excess of £40,000 a year, but many of the findings were applicable to other levels of management.

For the purpose of the research, 'role change' was defined as either a new role within the organization or a new job in a new company, or an individual who stays in a post but the structure within the organization or within the role has changed substantially.

The research highlights how dramatically the role of senior managers has changed during the past few years of continual organizational change. Managers, it was found, are more flexible and are changing roles frequently. Among the interesting facts to emerge from the survey were:

- The role of senior managers has changed significantly in the past two years. Sixty-two per cent of personnel directors and 74 per cent of role-changers said the change was substantial.

- Job moves at senior levels are now frequent. In over a third of organizations questioned, more than half of the senior management group had changed jobs in the past two years. At this level of seniority, across the whole sample, companies are filling 60 per cent of their vacancies with internal candidates.

- The majority of personnel directors think it takes six months to tell if someone will succeed in a changed role. However, the more senior the role the longer the time frame allowed. Personnel directors expressed concern that too many people are left to find their own way when earlier intervention in support of the transition could have made them more effective more quickly or avoided later problems. Role-changers felt success in a new role should be obvious after three months.

Looking at the motivators for role change, the research revealed:

- Senior executives appear to be taking a more sophisticated approach to career management than many personnel directors realize. When considering a new role, 81 per cent of role-changers now see it as a vehicle for career development. Over half also stated that other key considerations are the skills enhancement and the level of increased employability that the new role offers. This contrasts with the views of personnel directors, 84 per cent of whom believe that increased job challenge is the main motivator, although this was only rated as important by 63 per cent of role-changers.

- Fewer than 20 per cent of role-changers rated promotion, remuneration or enhanced status as a key motivator. This is in stark contrast to the personnel directors, around 75 per cent of whom believe that role-changers are motivated by recognition and remuneration, as well as career development.

On the question of support for role change, the research indicates:

- Where support for role change is offered it tends to take a traditional form of handover – induction and training courses.
- Role-changers did not see formal development processes as helpful, preferring tailored personal development programmes, coaching and mentoring.
- Role-changers strongly expressed the need for some 'older wiser counsel' and 'a safe ear' to whom they can talk openly and honestly.

Role-changers were not generally aware of the development opportunities open to them. There was a significantly lower take up of support and development by role-changers than personnel directors believe is provided. Twenty-two per cent of role-changers stated that they did not receive any support and development when they changed roles. Role-changers' requests for development appear to be influenced by what is known to be available within the organization rather than what they believe would be most helpful.

Forty-four per cent of role-changers believed that a specific role change programme would have enhanced their entry into the new role. However, only 7 per cent of companies questioned offered a specific role change programme.

Key contributors to successful role change were agreed by over 90 per cent of personnel directors and role-changers as:

- Clear indication of role needs
- Matching individual capabilities to the role specification
- Effective management of the entry stage by the individual
- Feedback provided by the organization
- Support by the line manager

- Monitoring of performance at the initial stages.

Asked what the essential elements should be in a role change programme, role-changers strongly identified networking, developing senior level relationships and awareness of self and impact on others. In general, when taking on a senior post, role-changers recognized the need to enhance personal skills, more than task and work-related skills. Organizations like 3M (see Chapter Ten) with their multi-source feedback systems appear to have anticipated these needs.

Examining the implications of the survey, GHN concludes: 'With flatter organizations, role change at senior levels is becoming more substantial. Promotion steps are larger. Cross-functional moves to develop a broader understanding of the business may require markedly different sets of skills, both personal and technical.

'The established assumptions about the support capable people need when taking on a new role need to be challenged. More may be required than the traditional induction and support from colleagues and boss, where time may now be limited.

'Organizations are recognizing the value to the business of getting role change right. Many are investing heavily in the selection stage. Career panels, development centres, competencies, psychometrics are being used to match individuals effectively to roles that have been clearly defined. However, the critical stage, effective management of the entry into a new role, is still left substantially to the individual and appears under-resourced.'

The demise of jobs
All this may be academic if the heretical views of William Bridges, the management guru and author of *Jobshift*, are to be taken seriously. He argues that it is pointless to think of careers any more in terms of jobs. He points out that 'we only started *having* jobs at the beginning of the eighteenth century; before that we *did* jobs, we didn't have them.'

It was only industry's need for efficient production that led to people having jobs, Bridges reminds us. In order to make a profit, businesses needed to operate like machines. Early industrial employees were simply unthinking operatives who served as efficient, non-mechanical machine parts. They were employed, as company resources, much the way any other resource is used by its owners.

Today, the talk is of the intelligent enterprise, knowledge workers and the centrality of information. Power is shifting from the all-seeing employer to individuals and teams with specialist expertise. Business has become far too complex to be run like a ship piloted in a clear and unequivocal direction. Employees now have to think for themselves; their intelligence is critical to defining the direction of the business. They are becoming partners and suppliers, not mere implementers of an omniscient manager's decisions.

While jobs are disappearing never to return, Bridges is careful to point out that work is still around. It is just that it can no longer be done in such discrete boxes. More and more work is done by teams in which everyone is expected to pitch in to help complete every part of a complex task. Pooling of effort and intelligence is so important now, in so many kinds of work, that it no longer makes sense to chop it up into the fixed chunks we call jobs.

Taking Bridges' views to their logical conclusion calls into question the whole future of organizations. The more organizations outsource their activities and establish new relationships with independent suppliers and sub-contractors, the more they call into question the need for organizations. If organizations are there to gather and process information (e.g. relaying information on consumer preferences to a myriad sub-contractors), the real question is for how much longer that 'middleman' role will be required. The falling cost and increasing globalization of information permits consumers to replace activities previously provided by organizations within the supply chain.

GHN lists six important aspects of managing in a world without jobs:

- *Select people on the basis of their suitability and desire to do the work* – not for their qualifications, past experience or where they come from.

- *Pay them fees of some sort and give them a share of the profits.* Tenure and seniority-based salaries are out.

- *Create new personnel policies.* Even core employees will become suppliers of services requiring special contracts, portable benefits and personal pensions. Today's personnel policies are obsolete: they focus too narrowly on permanent core workers while marginalizing more flexible, temporary workers. This attitude needs to shift 180 degrees. Leading-edge companies will create policies modelled to fit the flexible employee seen as a supplier of services.

- *Manage and motivate differently*: you cannot tell a strategic partner what to do. Often the best knowledge workers will be presenting you with proposals on how your business should progress. Your leadership may come down to deciding which of competing proposals are most worthy of your investment. Or it might be to coax extra commitment out of suppliers who could easily take their services elsewhere. This calls for leadership which is fully and finally divorced from the weight of positional authority.

- *Create a culture where it is OK to ask for help.* Provide access to external wisdom by encouraging networking. Offer both internal and external mentoring schemes. These will provide individuals with a personal coach as well as friendly support. If the mentor is external they will benefit from an objective sounding board.

- *Help 'employees' maintain their employability.* 'Employees' with no jobs to aspire to, only their own businesses to develop, need to learn how to create work for themselves. Creating work is an entrepreneurial task – not an old-fashioned government job creation scheme. Careers will now become more like the work histories of professionals such as doctors, lawyers or management consultants. Many 'staff' employees already see themselves as internal consultants. A career of this sort does not advance up a managerial hierarchy, but through a growing professional reputation.

Index